CONTENDING FOR THE FAITH

CHRISTIAN COUNSELING & SPIRITUAL WARFARE

Book One From The "Contending for the Faith Series."

By

Dr. Tom Knotts, JR.

www.SRA-DIDFreedomInChrist.Com

Prologue . . . A Message to the Counselors

NOTE: All the incidents in this book are true. In order to protect confidentiality, all the names and minor circumstances have been changed. Conversations have been restated to the best that memory permits surrounding the events that are mentioned.

Spiritual warfare is not a subject that is easily spoken about. It is a topic that most Christians want to know more about, but in conservative circles, they are too afraid to discuss. This is because there has been a great deal of damage done, to the cause of Christ in the area of spiritual warfare. The devil has used many well meaning individuals, in healing and deliverance ministries, to popularize and glamorize the concept of demonic oppression. These charlatans have been deceived by the devil. The true essence of spiritual warfare is in understanding what the Bible teaches on sin, the nature of angels and the cleansing power of Jesus Christ. Those who have been deceived are being used to spread deception. As I will show you, the things they do in public showmanship is something that is practiced in many cults around the world. There is the guiding rule; if anything contradicts the word of God then it is not of God.

There are many individuals that claim spiritual warfare is not biblical but it is my prayer that by the end of reading this book, you will see clear evidence from the Scriptures proving its reality and justifying its practice. Friends, all around us people are in bondage. They are being spiritually oppressed, and some are even being possessed. Christ has come to set the captives free.[1] That freedom is still freely offered. The blood of Jesus can cleanse us from every sin. May the Lord use the information given in this volume, to equip those challenged in counseling by, sometimes unexplainable circumstances brought on by an unseen world.

Let me make something very clear before we begin; the ministers of God need to be prepared before entering into the realm of spiritual warfare. You must be in close fellowships with the Lord God. The Bible is very clear; if we have hidden sin in our hearts, He, (God), will not hear us.[2] We must have hearts that are pure and strong, tempered in the things of God. If we are living with hidden sin in our lives or spiritual strongholds, than the work we do will be from our flesh. The Bible is very clear about dead works, they profit nothing.[3] Our life is not to be characterized, as one of ritual or just going through the motions. We must have a vibrant, living relationship, with the Lord Jesus Christ so that we are led by the Holy Spirit in our counseling ministries. Don't just go through the motions. There are many counselors out there that have training and knowledge but they are void of the love of Christ. They do not have compassion and empathy for those they work with. If you are not doing the work because you have a deep, passionate, love for

---

[1] Isaiah 58:1-11, 61:1
[2] Psalm 66:8
[3] 1 Corinthians 13:3

the Lord Jesus Christ, than you are working from the flesh. It should be your desire to draw closer to the Lord in order to be prepared for battle.

Don't mislead your clients; are you really a Christian Counselor?

Do you study the word of God so you can apply it to the individual?

Another point of consideration is this; if you do not know the word of God, than why do you call yourself a Christian Counselor? Just because you call yourself a Christian does not mean that you are a Christian Counselor. In the last twenty years I have had the privilege of meeting many counselors that do not know the Bible. If you asked them about gluttony they would begin by explaining obsessive compulsive disorders and different therapy approaches for dealing with the problem. Rather than turning to the Scriptures and showing the individual what the Bible teaches on excesses, such as gluttony, and then dealing with the sin of gluttony; they immediately turn to techniques that have been designed and developed from a world position that is void of Christ. That is not Christian Counseling. Being a Christian that counsels, does not automatically qualify you a *Christian counselor*.

First and foremost, a Christian counselor believes in the power of God to change lives. They have a strong conviction that the word of God is literal and true; all of God's word. I had a woman come to me that had been married five times and was secretly considering divorcing her current husband. While out shopping, she had met a man that she was attracted to and by the time she came to me, she had already been having an affair with him for over three months, while her husband was at work. I had just planted a church in this town and had a reputation for being a good counselor. She did not come to me because she was troubled over her affair; she came to me for advice on how to leave her husband, as he was a good man and she didn't want to hurt him. When she told me about her situation I informed her that she was committing adultery and that her actions were destroying, at least three lives. I informed her that her decisions would affect the lives of her entire family to include her children and grandchildren.

This would be a good time to mention that the man she was having an affair with, had been married to the same wife for over twenty two years. She told me that before her last divorce that she went to her pastor for advice and her pastor told her that in the matters of love, she needed to follow her heart, as God's first desire was for her happiness. I replied that, if that was the advice her former pastor had given her, that it was not only un- Biblical but actually went against the word of God. She got very upset at this statement and felt the need to defend her pastor. She began voicing her praise of just how wonderful the pastor was. I opened the Bible and showed her the following verse.

"The heart is deceitful above all things, and desperately wicked: who can know it?"[4]

I informed her that her heart would try to lead her into a sinful life and away from pleasing God. She then said. "But Jesus is in my heart!" I told her that God never contradicts his word. He actually gives us His word to be a guide and manual for our lives.

"All scripture is given by inspiration of God, and is profitable for doctrine, for reproof, for correction, for instruction in righteousness:"[5]

I then asked her to tell me about her salvation and how it was that she came to know the Lord. She told me that she had been baptized as an infant and confirmed at twelve years of age. I went on to explain to her that a church cannot confirm her as a child of God. We must come to God admitting that we are a sinner but also believing that Christ died for their sins. Christ shed his blood in order to cleanse us from all unrighteousness and that if she would call out to him for salvation he would come into her heart and give her eternal salvation. She prayed to receive the Lord as her Savior and the change was immediate. You could see from her face that God had cleansed her. We discussed the proper way to handle her situation; one that would obedient and that would glorify God. She went home and confessed to her husband what she had doing behind his back and then asked for his forgiveness. She also broke off the relationship with the other man

---
[4] Jeremiah 17:9
[5] 2 Timothy 3:16

and asked for his forgiveness. The last I heard she was still married to the same husband and living as God intends.

Friends, our goal is not to find ways for people to feel better about themselves, while living in the midst, of sinful life patterns. As counselors of God we need to confront sin with the Scripture's and then show the client how they can turn their life around so that it honors God and blesses them.

Do you believe in the power of sin, to destroy lives?

Do you also believe in the abundance of grace to cover that sin?[6]

Do you know the word of God well enough, to know when something is a sin?

The counselor of God should be in the word of God every morning. It is their meat and drink. It should be such a part of their life that flows through them.[7] A friend of mind once pronounced a blessing upon me. He said, "May your tongue have the speech of Eden." Our conversation should be such as becomes the things of heaven. They should be used to edify and build up others. This means that the conversations we have with others, should be leading them into a closer life of fellowship and devotion to Christ. It is from the abundance of the heart that the mouth will speak, let

---

[6] Romans 5:20
[7] Psalm 50:23; Ephesians 4:22; Philippians 1:27, 3:20; 1 Timothy 4:12; James 3:13; 1 Peter 1:15, 3:2; 2 Peter 3:1

your heart be filled with God's word.[8] May our hearts speak the things that become Christ.[9]

Do you practice what you teach?

Lastly friends, the counselor should also be a person that is characterized as living a righteous life. We should seek to live the gospel in our homes, our jobs in every place that we are found.[10] We live righteously not to be seen of men, but to honor God. Our Lord is watching over us all the time, he never sleeps and he never slumbers.[11] Our Christian life should be one characterized as being, one of a continual state of prayer.[12] It is the power of God that changes lives, not our intelligence or personalities. Our relationship with God should be identified by a deep love for God. This love should keep us in a continual state of prayer. It is a love relationship, with our dependence being solely upon Him.

When you entered the field of serving God as a counselor, the position you took was on the front lines in the war between the kingdom of darkness and light. You joined into a battle for the souls of men and woman. It is now your duty and calling, to help those who have been cast down and are being trampled upon by the enemy. Just as soldiers will pick up their fallen brothers in arms, lifting them up and carrying them back to a place of safely,

---

[8] Matthew 12:34; Luke 6:45; Acts 4:20
[9] 1 Corinthians 1:10, 2:13; Titus 2:1; 1 Peter 4:11
[10] James 1:22
[11]
[12] Acts 12:5; Romans 1:9; 1 Thessalonians 2:13, 5:17; 2 Timothy 1:3

so is the work of a counselor. We are called, the ministers of reconciliation.[13] This involves coming alongside a fallen brother or sister and then lifting them up before the Lord in prayer, offering to help bear their burdens so they can get back onto, the straight and narrow path of following Christ.[14] Friends we are all walking on the straight and narrow path and from time to time we will all fall. Sometimes it's hard to get up on your own and that's when a person can really use the help of a friend.

This world is a dark place; sometimes it's hard to keep our eyes on the road. Staying on this path can only be done in the light of God's revealed word. God's word is a lamp unto our feet and a light unto our path.[15] It is God's desire that we all walk in the light of Christ.[16] I remember when I first studied this concept, I was amazed to find out that during the days of Christ there was a small lamp that would attach to the front of the foot. In the dark of night it would give you just enough light to take your next step. It was designed to keep you on the road. If you took your time walking the lamp reveal obstacles or pitfalls in front of you enabling you to navigate around them. By using the foot lamp, the journeyer could walk in the darkest of night and stay on the straight and narrow road.

If our hearts focus is not on Christ; then our heart will lead us into sin. Innate desires will cause us to wander off the straight and narrow path and

---

[13] 2 Corinthians 5:8-19
[14] Galatians 6:1-10; Matthew 7:13; Psalm 140:5; 1 Timothy 3:7; 2 Timothy 2:26
[15] Psalm 119:105; Proverbs 6:23
[16] Isaiah 2:5; 1 John 1:7; Revelations 21:24

once we step onto the wayside, the cares of this world will begin to choke the life out of us. Many people slip and fall with the first step they take off the path. The sides of the narrow road can be just a step down with a gradual decrease in elevation that slowly leads you away from that path of righteousness. Sometime when a person steps off the road they find that they have stepped onto a slippery slope of sin making them unable to stand. They fall hard; many get the winded knocked out of them that when they need someone to reach down and help them up.

Many believers are challenged in their faith by unholy unions. By this I am talking about friendships and fellowships that are with unbelievers or worse, those that say they are Christians when they aren't. We need to make sure that those we fellowship with are truly seeking to live for God. If we yoke ourselves to unbelievers it will affect our Christian walk. To be friends with the world is to be the enemy of Christ.[17] The effects of an unholy union are best illustrated in the parable of the tare and the wheat.

Above the surface, a tare and a wheat plant look just a like when they are growing. They look just like they are both wheat plants but they are very different. Below the soil the tare plant will wrap around the root of the wheat plant and will then grow up alongside the wheat plant. This is because the tare cannot support itself against the elements of wind and rain. If it does not wrap around something else for support, it will fall to the ground and will grow horizontally along the ground until it can latch onto another plant. It

---

[17] 1 Corinthians 11:32; James 4:4

needs another plant to support it. Once a tare plant has attached itself to the wheat plant, its weight will pull the wheat plant at an angel so that it cannot get direct sunlight, which is the natural desire of the wheat plant. Not only will the tare miss-direct the wheat plant away from the direct rays of the sun but below the ground its roots will begin encircling the root of the wheat plant, continually growing tighter until it eventually cuts off the wheat plants abilities to receive the nutrients that it needs to live. When the time comes for both plants to produce their seeds, the tare will have completely killed the wheat plant by choking the life out of it. The tare plant will then consume what is left of the wheat plant. The tare plant will produce many seeds that are inedible but which very effective in spreading out over the surrounding area, repeating the process the next growing season. The tare chokes the life out of the wheat.

In the Christian life there are people that claim to be children of God but actually they are unsaved. They will cause the brother or sister to turn away from Christ. They will come up alongside of them, choking the life out of them until they die spiritually. As God's ministers of righteousness we are to be the ones to come alongside those, who have fallen. We need to take the time to help them untangle their lives from the cares of this world that are destroying their lives. We also need to confront the tares that come to us, showing them holding forth the truth of God's word, showing them the saving grace offered by God the Father in the person of Jesus Christ. Our hearts desire should be to help all that come to us so they too can walk the straight and narrow path of Christ. It is more than just being a Good Samaritan; it is being a holy priest of the higher calling.[18]

A Counselor should be given over to prayer

One thread that runs through all Christian ministries is this; the servant of God needs to have a heart that is devoted and true. One area of personal devotion is in the practice of regular times of prayer. This involves setting aside a time of personal prayer which includes fasting as the Lord leads. In this ministry you will encounter entities that will only come out of the person through prayer and fasting.[19] Friends, the demonic realm is real. A great deal of being a Christian Counselor happens in the sphere of spiritual warfare. When you help a person get free from sin, or spiritual strongholds, you are going to be involved in a spiritual warfare. The enemy will set his face against you, your family, and your finances; everything in your life will be a target.[20] That is why the life of a minister of God is not some nine to five job; it is a way of life, it is a calling of God.

A Christian Counselor is a holy priest of God

The world is filled with secular counselors that can tell a person all about the dynamics of the human body and what medications can help them to cope with their problems making life more manageable. They can

---
[18] Ezekiel 3, 33; Acts 20; Galatians 6:1; Luke 8, 10:33; Matthew 13:25; 1 Peter 2:5; Revelations 1:6, 5:10
[19] Matthew 17:21; Mark 9:29
[20] Luke 22:31

recommend therapies for coping with problems but there is a difference between coping and solving of problems. Only the Holy Spirit of God can convince a person of sin, righteousness and judgment. People are in need of cleansing and only the blood of Jesus can wash them clean. Many of the clients that you will see are in the midst of trials, struggles or sickness. Often these are the result of ungodly lifestyle choice they have made. Mental wards are filled with individuals suffering from illness all stemming from, either personal sins they have committed or sins that have been committed against them through another. I first heard this from a colleague in the prison ministry. At this time I was skeptical of the statement because I knew very little about spiritual warfare. When I counseled I relied upon techniques that were void of the power of God. They looked at everything from a medical position; the subject of sin, judgment and accountability were not a part of it. To illustrate his point about the effects of sin upon the mind of an individual, he entered into the mental wing of the facility and then as he walked down the middle of the ward he began preaching on how the blood of Jesus can cleanse us from all our sins. The reaction was incredible! The whole wing exploded with people screaming incredible obscenities, some fell to the floor thrashing, and others ran to the corners of their cells looking as if they were trying to hide from something. The staff had to escort him from the ward for his own safety. It took days before the inmates were settled back down.

Now I wan t you to understand that the patients did not act like this when we walked in and talked about anything else. As a matter of fact, most of them were quite able to communicate with us or the staff and did so routinely. But there was something strange about the way they reacted when he began preaching on the blood of Jesus Christ; it drove them into frenzy! This was not an isolated incident.

I worked as Senior Chaplin in a facility that housed only inmates that had served their time, but because of the nature of their crime, they could not be released back into society. These men were termed as habitual sexual predators. They were considered incurable. When I first started work in the facility I saw the violent reactions they would have to prayer or speaking on the blood of Jesus Christ. Many I could not work with face to face but only through bars or small windows as they were too unpredictable. But during my time there I counseled dozens of the individuals and saw the power of God to deliver them from powerful demonic strongholds. It happened by them confessing their sins and asking God to forgive them and to grant them salvation. I even had one man that became completely possessed, his eyes rolled back in his head and he was shaking violently. The voice that came out of his mouth said it was Legion. I bound it and he was able to speak again. I asked the Lord what he needed to confess and he told me that for thirty eight years he had been committing crimes against children and had moved through five different states. By confessing his sin and asking God for forgiveness he was set free. He even went before the judge and told him of over one hundred more crimes he had committed. He knew he would never be released if he confessed these crimes but it was the right thing to do. He told me later that he would be serving the rest of his natural life in jail but he was free at last.

When the facility was moved to another part of the state the Chief asked if I would be willing to move be the head Chaplain over the new facility. I had to decline the offer. The only reason why I was offered the position is because these men were changed by the power of God in cleansing their hearts and minds. The officers saw the change, the warden saw the change, the psychiatrists that did not believe in God saw the change; thought they could not explain the change. What I am saying is; through the confession of sin and asking of forgiveness many of these men were changed. It was witnessed by all those around them and it could only have been done by the power of God.[21]

Friends, people need to be told the truth. A child of God cannot live as it once had. It is not of the world any longer but is of the Kingdom of the living God. We as holy priest of the living God are to minster to those that come to us for cleaning. We are to lift them up before God and to be the vessel that God uses to reveal his word and power to them. When a person comes to Christ for salvation they need to know that they are no longer a child of the devil; they are a child of God and this world is not their home any longer. A child of God will not fit in with the world and the world will never be able to satisfy them. Only by returning to God can a person find

---

[21] Matthew 22:29; Mark 12:24; Luke 9:43; Romans 1:16; 1 Corinthians 1:18, 24, 2:5, 2 Corinthians 6:7, 13:4; 2 timothy 1:8; 1 Peter 1:5

rest to their souls. It is only through abiding in Christ that a person can have the peace and rest they are so desperately seeking for.[22]

The Conclusion

The reality is this; since sin entered into the human race, life has been hard; it is a struggle. Peace was taken from us, in that one single act of rebellion by Adam. The world in which we now live, is a chaotic and sinful place. But Jesus Christ can give us peace in the midst of these storms. We have an enemy whose desire is to damn mankind. He seeks to do this by keeping people from coming to personally knowing the Savior. If that does not work and the person does come to salvation, the enemy will then seek to ensnare them and entangle them in a life of sin. He will seek to separate them from the power of God in their life.[23]

Let me ask you this; are you a counselor of God? Will you tell them of the love of Jesus Christ?

This same enemy sets himself against those that do know the Savior, He spares no effort in seeking to tear them down. He wants to destroy their lives. Will you stand with those in need? It is not God's will for his children to be ignorant of the schemes of the devil.[24] Christian Counselors need to be able to recognize, when we, or someone that comes to us, is under demonic

---

[22] Isaiah 30:15; Luke 15; Matthew 11:29; Isaiah 30:15; 2 Corinthians 5:17; John 8:44
[23] Isaiah 59:1-3, ff. ; Ephesians 4:26-30, (30)
[24] 2 Corinthians 2:11; Ephesians 6:11; 1 Timothy 3:6-7; 2 Timothy 2:26; 1 John 3:8-10

attack or the influence of the enemy. We can do all things through Christ Jesus, Who strengthens us.[25] May the Lord strengthen you in Christ Jesus as you endeavor to work for Him; In Christ's love: Dr. Tom Knotts, Jr.

---

[25] Philippians 4:13

OUTLINE

1   Spiritual Warfare ………………………………….. 19

2   Praying On The Armor …………………………….. 57

3   Generational Curses ………………….………....... 78

4   Un-holy Ties and Attachments…………………..…..97

5   Weddings, Vows, and Summoning…………..………125

6   The Hidden Enemy………………………………...145

7   A Basic Guideline of Spirits...………………………174

8   A Short Word On DID ………….…………………..207

SPIRITUAL WARFARE . . .

I took upon the work, of writing this book for one reason; counselors are in need of training in spiritual warfare. For the past several years, I have spent a considerable amount of time in traveling the country, to train counselors in the art of spiritual warfare. Hermeneutics is the science and art of Biblical interpretation; it is the science of how to study the Bible. In the twenty plus years of college I was never taught about spiritual warfare. The subject was never brought up. It was not until I began Pastoring that I heard the term from a colleague. It was like some form of hidden taboo that was so shameful, the subject was completely avoided. As I began learning about what the Bible teaches it occurred to me; the Christian world had forgotten about the power of God to work in and through his people for healing and cleansing. I have found that there was a stigma attached to the subject of spiritual warfare. It was like, if a person believes in SW,[26] than they must be illiterate of not trained in field of psychology. The subject of spiritual oppression and possession was like a fairy tale. If you take the time to do the research you will find that many fairy tales, myths and legends had their basis in fact.

Friends, psychology literally means the study of the soul. I ask you this; who knows more about the soul than God? Colleges will teach students

---
[26] SW is the abbreviation for spiritual warfare

on the basic of human anatomy, the development of the mind and brain function but, rarely do they ever touch upon the subject of spiritual warfare. My first degree was in theology. I remember asking the head of the theology department why there was no mention of demon or demonic influence in the study of angelology and he told me that; "Once a person is saved the devil cannot influence them. Demons are a thing for the unsaved world." This man was well respected in his field possessing a solid doctorate in theology; but he was very wrong! Friends, what he believed was not only a wrong understanding, on what the Bible teaches about angelology, hamartiolgy and soteriology,[27] but it showed a complete ignorance of the basic Bible teaching on the three enemies of the believer. My purpose in writing this book is to educate Christian counselors everywhere on the subject of spiritual warfare so they can be properly equipped to meet the needs of those that come to them.

This is a time of great spiritual oppression. Because of the abundance of sin the hearts of many have grown cold. The spiritual oppression of the believer is ever increasing along with the sin of this generation.

As never before, the church of Christ is being approached by individuals needing healing and deliverance from just about every sin and ailment you can think of and some you never should. The attack upon the

---

[27] Angelology is the study of angels and demons; hamartiolgy is the study on sin; soteriology is the study of salvation and the atonement.

family has reached a proportionate all time high. Because of the abundance of sin things we used to take for granted, like safety, friendliness and open honesty have disappeared. Children are afraid to walk in public alone; and rightly so, evil is rampant. You cannot trust people anymore. This world is filled with demonized and evil people. Neighbors living next to each other for years do not even know each other. They are afraid to talk. They just go into their homes and lock the doors behind them. Because of the hardening of human heart our society has become increasingly more withdrawn and introverted.

    I was amazed, when in 1997, as I was sitting through a seminar on adult and child survivors of abuse,[28] the instructor made the statement, that this was the most medicated generation that has ever existed and also the most violent. To be honest I found it hard to believe. I had become jaded in my small town setting and was not in touch with the reality of how most people are living. I began researching the subject and found that the instructor was telling the truth; it was reported that over sixty percent of our society was on some form of medication. The range of those being treated was from adolescents to the elderly. To be technical even many of the children that are still in the womb are under the influence of some type of mood altering medications and/or drug that their mothers are taking. Even the fluoride in our drinking water affects the developmental process of the brain, making the drinker more docile and submissive towards authoritarian control. We live in a society that is plagued with a plethora of spiritual and

---

[28] It was a course through the APA

psychological illnesses. I believe the root to a great deal of these problems is the direct result of sin and/or spiritual oppression. Rather than confronting the person's sin or praying to lift the spiritual oppression, the conventional method is to offer a prescription. Once again, the instructor was correct; never before in American society has there been such a *"medicated"* generation.

Where is the power of God, Where is the joy of the Lord, and where is the church in all of this?

Here is where I am going with this; many born again believers are living on anti-depressants, alcohol, or mood inhibitors/controllers. Friends, as born again believers, our dependence is to be upon the Lord Jesus Christ; not medications. It seems that society has forgotten about the power of God. Christ is the source of our strength. He has given us the Comforter to help us cope with lives problems. I have sat through seminars where the Christian instructor felt the need to justify referring people for medications; stating that the time we live in calls for it. He said we have to come out of the Stone Age and learn to roll with the flow. Man doesn't have to live with stress any longer. According to this man, the only reason God healed and delivered in the days of Christ was because they did not have a medical alternative. Now with the advances in medical science and the availability to prescription drugs; anxieties and problems are a thing of the past.

My friend this philosophical approach to life is not based on truth. It is an affinity with the world that is void of Christ. During the days of Christ, drugs were more than readily available to those that wanted them. This was the full time occupation of sorcerers and alchemists;[29] they had a myriad of topical compounds and elixirs that would change moods or inhibit feelings and emotions. They had drugs to stop anxiety and potions to make you sleep at night. These methods are limited in that they only treat the symptom; they did not cure the problem. But this was not the way to deal with the root of the problem. The Key to bringing a person to wholeness is to find the root of their problem and then to address whatever the problem is, Biblically. In extreme cases of lunacy or demonic oppression/possession, the person will need to be set free and this is the job of the church.[30] I found many cases of this in the prison system.

I referred earlier to a Christian instructor who justified the worldly approach to changes in technology and advancements in medicine. Another one of his main points was that the world that we live in is very different today. But this also is not completely true. Yes, I will agree technology has changed but people have not. Since the fall of man in the Garden of Eden all men have been plagued with trials and tribulations. There has always been two ways that people dealt with their problems; they either turn to the Lord for help, or they turn to the world. Look back at just the last hundred years and you will find this to be true. Have you ever heard of the great

---

[29] Acts 8:9, 13:6-8
[30] Mark 1:27, 3:11, 5:13, 6:7, 9:38; Luke 9:49, 11:14; Matthew 10:1; Acts 5:16, 8:7

depression? How about World War I or II? Throughout all of the earth's history there have always been trials and tribulations. How do you think the world felt when it was conquered by Alexander the Great, or Caesar? The way God's children handled the stress of life in the past was to turn to God. Life has always been filled with stress and sin. Technology may have changed but people are still the same. We love, laugh, cry, etc. we are human. God understands our humanity and he has given us his word and the indwelling of His Holy Spirit, Who is the Comforter to walk with us through all of the trials of life. In times past, the church took the stand that by seeking to live righteously a person would experience the peace of God. This was true even when they were being imprisoned or cast into a den of lions.[31]

Christian counseling is discipling the individual in right living

If a person can settle in their heart that they are going to live for God and then have peace with their decision, the burdens and stress of life will be lifted from their shoulders. The stress is removed because when you yoke yourself to Christ, the work of taking care of you and your family is placed upon Him. You simply walk with God and learn of him. He carries the burden and your load becomes light and easy to bear.[32] You can trust in the promises of God.[33] This brings up a good question. Why is it that many pastors have quit preaching against sin and the responsibility to live right? A

---

[31] Daniel 6; 1 Corinthians 15:32, 15:9; Galatians 1:13
[32] Matthew 11:29; 1 Peter 5:7
[33] Romans 9:4, 15:8; 2 Corinthians 1:20, 7:1; Galatians 3:6, 21; Hebrews 6:12, 8:6, 11:33; 2 Peter 1:4

home founded upon living for God can whether all of the storms of life. Problems occur when a Christian tries to live like the world. When a person turns away from the Lord, they have no other recourse but to turn medications in order help with their problems. If counselors were properly trained in:

a) Sin and its consequences
b) The word of God and how it applies
c) The art of living right before God and amongst men
d) How to confront others in love
e) How to lead someone to recognize when they are in sin
f) How to lead others to repentance
g) How to establish and maintain a life of devotion
h) Helping their clients to understand their role in the church
i) What fullness of life really it

If Pastor's and Christian Counselors turned back to the roots of Christianity there would be a great deal more joy of the spirit in the lives of believers and the love of Christ would be reaching our communities. Secular training that is void of the knowledge and power of God will blind a Counselor to the roots of spiritual problems. It's time for the church and its members to turn back to utilizing the Scriptures, and to trusting the Holy Spirit in revealing the root of what is causing a client's problems. Medication is not the solution to spiritual problems. It will not solve the problem it only makes it so the person can live with the problem.[34] Let me give you an example.

Not too long ago I took my car in for servicing. After working on my car the mechanic could not figure out why my brake light was stuck on. The light was not on before he worked on it but after repairing and replacing most of the entire front end, the light would not go off. He said that it was just a fluke that it came on while he was working on the car and that it must have been a bad sensor switch. He then replaced the switch but it did not make the light go off. He told me that I must have a bad light switch or a problem in the electronic relay somewhere and that it was not his fault and not worth my time to worry about. He said that he could disconnect the wiring to the light or that I could cover the dash light it with tape so that it would not bother me when I was driving. (Yes, this actually happened!) I took the car to another mechanic who inspected the car and told me the person who had done my rebuild had forgotten to put back on the car two very important magnetic strips that were located on the back of the sensors. He said that was why the light would not shut off. He also said that it would cause the anti lock braking system to cause the front end to shake when I used the brakes since it was not reading properly. It was shaking when I used the brakes. He said I should take it back to the original mechanic and tell him what he said. He even printed out a diagram of the front end assembly

---

[34] In cases where there is a physical reason for the problem, such as in thyroid problems or imbalances in the body due to genetics, injuries, or some other reason than medications are needed to bring back balance to the persons' body and mind. There are legitimate reasons for medications. But if the problems is from sin or cannot be medically explained than the root may be from spiritual oppression.

and circled the two parts that were missing so they mechanic would not have trouble identifying the parts. He did stress that he hoped the other mechanic did not through away the parts as they were quite expensive pieces.

I took the car back to the original mechanic and showed him the diagram and he said; "O'I through those away. I didn't think they were important." Those two little pieces cost over $500.00 dollars to replace, labor not included. Without those two little magnetic strips the sensors would not work right and the brakes would continually grab and release as I drove the car. Because he did not know what the problem was, he thought that I should just live with the problem as it was not that bad on the brakes. To keep the dash light from bothering my conscious he recommended disconnecting the wiring or covering the light with a piece of tape. Had I of allowed him to do that it would have caused my brakes to wear out prematurely while also lessening the braking power of the car. I can't imagine that the front end shaking wasn't also hard on the ball joints and other front end parts. The car was not designed to function properly without those two little magnetic strips. The lights were there to tell me that something was wrong with the car.

Anxiety or depression is not the problem; it is simply the light that is telling you something is wrong. Something is either, missing, disconnected or broken. How can a counselor deal with a person's problems if they don't understand it? The mechanic did not understand the design of my car and so he threw away two very important, little magnetic strips. A little sin can do a great deal of damage in a person's life. It is the little foxes that run along the top of the grape vines that cause the clusters of grapes to get knocked off the vine and ruined and sometimes it is the little things in life that keep us from experiencing and producing the fruit of the spirit in our life.[35] Because he was unable to detect what the problem was, he offered to me what he considered to be the next best solution. Had I of followed his advice the problem would have still been there and it would have created many more problems. He had good intention and was a very kind person but his good intentions did not qualify him for the job he was doing. He was certified and licensed for working on automobiles but he still did not know what he was doing in that area of mechanics. He offered a solution that would not remove the problem but it would attempt to take my mind off of the problem.

Sadly, many counselors simply do not know how to find the root of their client's problems. Too many rely upon the methodology of the world rather than the indwelling of the Holy Spirit. Simply put, counselors are not being trained in how to trust in the Spirit of God to work in their clients. Christ is the Wonderful Counselor and His Spirit will speak to his child revealing the cause of their problems.[36] Allow me to give you an example.

Identity what is physical and what is spiritual

If a person comes to you with a burn on their arm seeking help and guidance from you, the best approach to take, would be in sending them to the hospital. At the hospital they have qualified physician's who have at

---

[35] Song of Solomon 2:15; Galatians 5:22-ff.
[36] Isaiah 9:6; John 16:13, 23; 1 John 2:27

their disposal all the equipment necessary to properly fix the person's arm. Things affecting the physical body need to be treated accordingly. Their problem was they had received a burn. The body is not made to be burned. When the person received the burn it took away the body's ability to experience peace and rest. It needed to be cleaned and bandaged and then allowed a period of time for healing. While in the healing stage the body had to fight off such things as infection, disease, predators, (if the person is located in the unprotected wild.) The body will even have to fight the mental urge to scratch the affected area, as that would only make it worse. The tangible realm needs to be dealt with accordingly. You get a splinter, you pull out the splinter. This is right, proper and effective. This is common sense. Common sense is lost, when a person is having a problem stemming from the spirit and it is dealt with from the physical.

So, why are we so quick to deal with spiritual issues from a physical approach? If a person is having a spiritual problem, than wouldn't that necessitate a spiritual solution? Yes, it is true that the body can affect our mental position but let us not over look the fact that our minds also greatly affect our bodies. It has been shown that depression is a natural occurrence of the grieving process after a person experiences loss. Losses take many forms. It can be the unexpected death of a loved one, the loss of a career, the loss of an ability or limb. Depression and anger are a natural part of the grieving process and are a natural part of living the Christian life. Problems occur if the depression or anger persist or evolve into other emotional problems. God certainly knows that we are going to go through period of depression but it is not the will of God for his child to remain in a state of depression.[37] A life that is impaired through depression or medication is not glorifying to God. It sends a message to the world that the God we serve is impotent; and my friend that is a lie from the pit of hell. We serve a God that is all powerful. Through our God we overcome the world.[38]

What a person believes will affect every aspect of their life

The power of a mind is incredible. The way that a person thinks will affect their entire being; mind, body, soul and spirit. What a person believes to be true, will even direct the way in which they live. It has been proven that people can make themselves sick simply by believing that they are going to be sick. There are even cases where people have died because they wanted to die. They lost all hope along with their desire to live. The mind shuts down the body's ability to live. Just like a wound or a splinter will war, against the body's ability to have peace and rest, there are spiritual things that are constantly waging a war against the individual. This is spiritual warfare!

Spiritual warfare is an attack against a person spirit

A majority of Christian counseling is spent dealing with depression. I have been asked by many people; *"Where is the joy of the Spirit promised in*

---

[37] Jonah 4, (9)
[38] 1 Chronicles 29:11; Psalm 98:1; Isaiah 25:8; 1 Corinthians 15:55, 57; 1 John 5:4

the Scriptures?" Joy is the primary target of the enemy. The Devil knows that if he can steal a person's joy, he can also steal their strength. The joy of the Lord is our strength.[39] Strength is defined as; *"the power to resist force…the power to resist attacks."*[40] Our ability to resist the attacks of the enemy are substantially weakened by a loss of joy. Our joy is directly linked to our commitment to God. This is why the Bible tells us to take up the shield of faith; it is so we can withstand the fiery darts of the wicked.[41] Faith is a commitment to God. It is this commitment to God that enables us to withstand the things in life that will make us inflamed. This term for fiery darts, literally means, the things which cause us to become inflamed. It is a term that is used for the melting down of metals in order to separate the various components. On one hand, it is a purifying process through separating the dross from the metal but it is also a proving of the metal. The extreme heating of the metal will prove the purity of the metal.[42] But on the other hand, if the metal is over heated, i.e. inflamed the metal will it begin to breakdown and become consumed by the flame. As a young man I wanted to find a way to move aluminum cans for recycling that was less bulky. It would take my dad's truck to move all of the bags I would save up so I thought if I could melt them into a solid block I could store up a bunch of blocks and then take them all in at the same time. I build a fire in the backyard and then began throwing the cans in. I quickly learned that if the

---

[39] Nehemiah 8:10
[40] Merriam Webster; Webster's New Collegiate Dictionary; G.&C.Merriam Co., Publishers Springfield, Mass., USA
[41] Ephesians 6:16
[42] Malachi 3:2-3

fire was too hot it would consume the cans rather than melting them into a solid block. I burned up about thirty pounds of cans!

The wicked things in this world seek to break us down. They want to consume us. It is the goal of the world, our own flesh and the devil to try and break us down and to destroy out life. These three enemies work together in this effort to destroy us. It is the joy of the Lord that gives us the ability to withstand these attacks leveled against us. The loss of joy can affect every area of life. This is what makes joy a primary target of the enemy.

The gift of joy is listed second, only to love, in the fruits of the spirit.[43] It holds second place, because a person cannot experience true joy without the love of God in their life. The Greek word for love is *agape*. The word agape speaks about a love, for someone or something that is so passionate that it drives the person to serve the object of their affection. It causes you to want to make them happy. Friends, we love the Lord Jesus Christ because he first loved us.[44] It was this love that God has for us that drove him to leave the splendors of heaven, to come and die for us on the cross of Calvary. He, who knew no sin, became sin for us, so that we could be made the righteous of God in him.[45] Once you've experience the love of God, you are never the same. He fills you with a love for himself and for others. He gives you peace and joy like you have never had before. It is this love that gives you the joy of the Lord and the fruit of the Spirit. The fruit of the Spirit is in all goodness, righteousness and truth. It is the foundation for

---

[43] Galatians 5:22; Ephesians 5:9
[44] 1 John 4:19
[45] John 3:16; 2 Corinthians 5:21

living the Christian life. If the enemy takes a persons' joy it affects every aspect of the fruit of the Spirit in their life. This in turn will hinder their ability to live out the goodness, righteousness and truth of God. What many believers do not understand is that their ability to lead others to salvation in Christ comes as a direct result of their having joy in the Lord.

> "Behold, God is my salvation; I will trust, and not be afraid: for the LORD JEHOVAH is my strength and my song; he also is become my salvation. Therefore ***with joy*** shall ye draw water out of the wells of salvation."[46]

Others will come and drink of the water of life that flows through you giving them a thirst for the truth and a desire to have the same saving power that you have experienced, for themselves. Your joy is a primary target of the enemy because his desire is to dame others. It is to keep them thirsty and dry so he can continually offer them the things of this world, things that will never satisfy. To do this he needs to cut them off from every resource that can bring them deliverance. When you came to salvation, the Lord took you, a vessel that was empty and made only to wash the filth of the earth off of peoples feet, and he filled you with new wine; the wine of the Holy Spirit. At that moment you became a vessel that could be used to bring joy to all those called to the marriage feast. The first miracle that God did in your life was to transform you, from an

---

[46] Isaiah 12:2-3

empty earthen vessel into a vessel that was filled with the greatest wine ever produced; a vessel that others would draw from to taste and see that the Lord is good. You became the dwelling place of the Comforter, the indwelling of the Holy Spirit of God that now began the work of producing all the fruit of the spirit in your life.[47] It is your joy in the Lord that allows others to draw from the waters of life. It is the word of your testimony that overcomes the world and offers all those that are thirsting for the truth, that there is mercy, forgiveness and fullness of life in Christ Jesus. I know that if you are truly a born again child of God it is your desire to see souls saved. If you want to be a vessel that leads others to salvation the power of God will be administered to others through your joy in the Lord. It is this abundance of life within you, the Holy Spirit of God that makes you a well of water springing up into life eternal.[48]

When a person looses the joy of the spirit the natural response is to turn to the leading of the flesh instead of the leading of God. I have known many counselor that have begun their ministries, being led by the Holy Spirit only to grow comfortable in the ministry that they had committed themselves to. They begin trusting in their own methodology with the conventional wisdom of man rather than relying on the Holy Spirit of God to speak to the counselee's mind and heart. Christ is the Wonderful Counselor; we can trust in his power to set the person free. What we ***should never***

---

[47] Matthew 2; John 14:6
[48] John 4, (14)

forget is that the work is God's, not ours. We are simply a vessel that the Lord has chosen to work through.

As Christian Counselors, God's Word is to be our sole source of guidance for life; that is what we offer the individuals we are working with. I am not suggesting that we do not need training or seminars; what I am saying is this; our reliance must be on knowing the truth of God's Scriptures and trusting in the power of the living God to change the person's heart and mind. When a counselor turns to the world and its methods, they will lose the power of God in their ministry. To be friends with the world, is to be the enemy of God[49] and my friend, only God, not the world can set the heart free and truly heal the mind and body. The enemy of our soul will try to blind the counselor to this fact and will lead them to ungodly devices.

The opposite of joy is depression which is usually defined as; "a low period in one's life or an emotional state marked by sadness, inactivity, or difficulty in thinking clearly. It often results in feelings of helplessness, hopelessness, a sense of rejection, and pessimistic or negative thoughts."[50] These are not conditions that the believer in Christ should be living with.

Depression can have many causes:
    a. A lack of rest

    b. Anger that has been turned inward

    c. A brain or physical injury

---

[49] 1 John 2:15-17, 4:3-5, 4:9
[50] How To Deal With Depression, — Dr. Preston T. Bailey, Jr. ; International School for Biblical Counseling , Advanced Warfare 1 Course 2

d. Biological reasons created by Demonic influences
   e. Seasonal influences, such as in the Arctic Circle where there are months with no darkness or months where there is no sunlight.[51]

Certainly there are many legitimate reasons for occasional bouts with depression but when depression persists, it is a problem that needs to be dealt with. Salvation is not to be endured, it is to be enjoyed.

Christ has come to set us free from the things which seek to shackle or bind us.[52] The idea of depression is something weighing or pressing down, hence depressing it, which leads us to the subject of spiritual depression. The Church has fallen asleep in dealing with spiritual depression. It is time for the church to stand up and shout, *"Awake thou that sleepest and redeem the time!*[53] Life is much too short for a believer in Christ to be spending years on medications when their freedom has already been purchased with the blood of our Lord Jesus Christ. The victory has already been won and someday we shall rest as the Lord has promised us[54] but let us not be naïve. The enemy of our Lord is still very active in working against the kingdom of Christ.

In Acts 14: 22 we read:

---

[51] This type of depression is called SAD, seasonal affective depression
[52] Luke 4:18; Isaiah 61:1
[53] Ephesians 5:14
[54] Hebrews 4:3-5

> "Confirming the souls of the disciples, and exhorting them to continue in the faith, and that we must through much tribulation enter into the kingdom of God."

Satan has a desire to steal the joy of the believer. He has a design in progress to ensnare and cause the child of God to become entangled in sin so that they are not able to walk in harmony with the Holy Spirit of God. But my friends once again I say, "The victory is already won!"[55]

As children of God, we need to claim the promises of God and to go forward in the power and the leading of the Holy Spirit. Thousands have been deceived by the enemy. Many Saints have fallen. The battlefield is littered, with failed ministries and shattered lives, of those who have given up contending for the faith that was once delivered unto them.[56] Many have become ensnared with the sins that so easily beset us;[57] this should not be. Salvation is not something to be endured until we reach heavens gates. No, salvation is to be enjoyed in the present. The eternal life God gives us begins here on earth not after we die. We will often become weary in the fight but never let us be weary of the fight. He, [Christ], has come to give us life and that means a life filled with joy while here on earth, just as it shall also be in heaven. The Bible very plainly teaches in 2 Corinthians 3:17 about the freedom afforded us in Christ.

---

[55] 1 Corinthians 1:15:57; 1 John 5:4
[56] Jude 1:3
[57] Galatians 5:1; 2 Peter 2:20; Hebrews 12:1

> "Now the Lord is that Spirit: and where the Spirit of the Lord is, there is liberty."

Friends, we need to be living in the freedom that Christ has purchased for us, with his own precious blood. One essential aspect of the counseling ministry is this;

When we find someone taken captive by the enemy, we work to see them set free.[58]

If we find someone who has given up because they were over burdened then let us do the work of Galatians chapter six and help them bear that burden. This is the ministry of Christ and it is the duty of a Christian. We should seek to restore the fallen brother or sister, back into a proper relationship with Christ. A person that has been beaten down by the world needs to be restored in the spirit of love. This is why as God's counselors we study His word; it is so that we can reassure others of the promises that God has given us in His word.[59] These promises are real. I have met many counselors that do not believe in the power of God. They did not believe that we could literally hold God accountable to keep the promises of His word. As a Christian Counselor, it is not enough to read the word of God; you must believe God's word is true. Those that come to us must see that we stand on the promises of Christ our King and that we are fighting the good fight of the

---

[58] Galatians 6:1
[59] 2 Timothy 2:15; 1 Peter 3:15

faith. We are to be contending for the faith. It is not commonly known, but D. Martin Lloyd Jones was a very effective Biblical counselor. Jones once said,

"There can be no doubt but that the condition known as spiritual depression is a very common complaint, indeed the more one thinks about it and the more one speaks about it, the more one discovers how common it is. We are considering this condition because, as I have suggested, there are at least two great reasons for our doing so. The first is that it is very sad that anybody should remain in such a condition. But the second reason is still more serious and important, that is that such people are very poor representatives of the Christian faith. As we face the modern world with all its turmoil and with all its difficulties and sadness, nothing is more important than that we who call ourselves Christian, and who claim the Name of Christ, should be representing our faith in such a way before others, as to give them the impression that here is the solution, and here is the answer. In a world where everything has gone so sadly astray, we should be standing out as men and woman apart, people characterized by a fundamental joy and certainty in spite of conditions, in spite of adversity."[60]

---

[60] Spiritual Depression Its Causes and Its Cure, D. Martin Lloyd – Jones ; pg. 23; Wm. B. Eerdmans Publishing Co. Grand Rapids, Michigan

D. Martin Lloyd Jones was a contender for the faith. He understood the power of Jesus Christ in setting souls free and restoring the spirit. Jones practiced Spiritual warfare.

When people discuss what spiritual warfare is there are many different ideas on the subject but spiritual warfare plainly defined is this; hindering the advances of Satan's kingdom and then obeying the command of our Lord to confront the kingdom of darkness and take back the ground that has been given to the enemy.

> "And I say also unto thee, That thou art Peter, and upon this rock I will build my church; and the gates of hell shall not prevail against it."[61]

It is very common for believers to be in the midst of spiritual warfare and not even know it. When feelings of depression or suicidal thoughts come over a person for no apparent reason, or a person is having a wonderful day but as soon as they walk into their home they feel overwhelmed with anger or rage; it is a clear indication that they are under the attack of the enemy! Whether they like it or not they are involved in spiritual warfare! Our joy is a gift from the living God; a gift that the enemy seeks to steal from us. In order to prevent this we must be prepared to identify the methods of warfare that the enemy is waging against us. This is accomplished by knowing the truth found in God's word. We must be able to rightly divide the word of God.

---

[61] Matthew 16:18

> "Study to show thyself approved unto God, a workman that needed not to be ashamed, rightly dividing the word of truth."[62]

It is through experiencing the truth of God in our life that we go through the process of being set free.[63]

Bank tellers are trained by studying legitimate money. By them becoming used to real currency, they developed the ability to recognize a counterfeit bill. There is an incredible lesson of truth that can be learned by the believer. By continually being in the word of God, we learn about God and how He works within His creation. The more familiar we are with the word of God the easier it will be for us to identify when the enemy is present and at work.

> "But strong meat belonged to them that are of full age, even those who by reason of use have their senses exercised to discern both good and evil." [Hebrews 5:14]

Historians tell the story of John Bunion the puritan preacher of grace. They said he would exhort his listeners to read the word of God by telling them that they must be beavers of the Bible if they were to build a home on God's

---

[62] 2 Timothy 2:15
[63] John 8:32

word. May this be the desire of our hearts and may our homes be built upon the word of God.

The enemy will try to separate us in order to conquer us

The enemy will attack our joy as believers. The enemy will also try to separate us from other believers and from fellowshipping with the Lord Jesus Christ. There is a strategic tactic that the enemy has been using since the beginning of man; it's called divide and conquer. For instance, the apostle Paul warns the church that after he leaves them, grievous wolves are going to enter in, not sparing any of the flock.[64] He was telling them that the church would come under attack in order to divide the members in order to attack the individual members. He likened the employed method to a pack of wolves that will drive the flock apart, separating the weaker sheep in order to pick off them off one by one. The enemy has used this method since the beginning of time. You may ask the question; "Why does the enemy continually use this tactic?," Because it works. Satan and his minions will stop at nothing to keep you from having a close relationship with the Lord Jesus Christ. As long as we are walking closely to the Lord Jesus Christ we are not going to be as likely to stray off the path of righteousness. We will also be in an attitude of prayer, lifting all our needs and concerns up to the Lord every day, while expecting him to work in our lives. There are many things that can try and separate our focus off of the Lord. I have known good

---

[64] Acts 20:29

men and woman that would never let a trial or personal tragedy separate their walk with the Lord. But then I have also seen those same individuals receive a promotion at work or win the lottery and their entire Christian walk and testimony became destroyed. By receiving something, that could have been an incredible source of blessing, because it took their focus off of Christ, it became a terrible curse to them. You would think that they would have been praising God for the blessing they had received, but they didn't. Instead they allowed the promotion to make them too busy to attend church, thus hindering their Christian walk and growth and affecting their testimony. I watched as it happened and even warned them of what I was witnessing but it only fell on deaf ears. They were too caught up in the experience.

It happened slowly. The family begin by missing church services. We had four services a week where I was Pastoring and they were attending three of them a week; every week. The first time they missed was on a Wednesday evening service. Then they began missing Sunday evening service until finally they were missing every other Sunday morning service as well. It did not just affect their attendance to worship. I went to visit the man and found that the family had quit reading their Bibles and praying together daily. Daily family worship is something I have always held to. After a few months they quite coming to church altogether. Eventually they were drawn back to their old ways and habits as prior to their salvation.[65] I did not see them until eight months later when the man called to ask if I would bail him out of jail. He had lost his job, began drinking and had

---

[65] Proverbs 14:14; Jeremiah 3:6,8,11-12,14,22, 8:5, 31:22, 49:4; Hosea 4:16,11:7, 14:4

become abusive to his wife. He went to jail and ended up getting divorced. He asked me how everything could have gone so wrong. I told him when he took his eyes off the Lord and went back into the world he became another casualty of spiritual warfare. We all fail, we all make mistakes, what is important is that we know that we can always come back to our heavenly father. His mercy and grace are all sufficient to cover our needs and the blood of Christ will always cleanse us from all of our sins. The god of this world will give you a promotion or even a kingdom if that is what it will take to get your worship and fellowship away from the true Lord God.

Why is it so important that we have a strong walk with the Lord? Satan knows that if he can sever your daily time with the Lord that he will begin limiting the power of God in your life.[66] Willful sin in a believer's life causes fear, anxiety and stress.[67] This is one of the main reasons ***anxiety disorders*** are so common among Christian believers. By not obeying the Scriptures and giving our cares to the Lord we will quickly become over loaded and unable to cope with stress. A prime directive of the believer is found in Philippians 4: 6 - 7 where the believer is instructed to not be anxious about anything but rather to trust God, giving our cares and burdens over to him.

> "Be careful for nothing; but in everything by prayer and supplication with thanksgiving let your requests be made known unto God. And the

---

[66] James 4:2-8; Isaiah 59:1-3
[67] Hebrews 10:26-27

peace of God, which passeth all understanding, shall keep your hearts and minds through Christ Jesus."

It has never been the intention of the Father for us to worry or to be stressed; stress kills! Stress causes incredible strains upon the body and the mind. It can cause undo weight gain, memory problems, hypertension, heart strain, and nervous disorders to name a few. By us not casting off our burdens and releasing them to the Lord they will weigh us down and hinder our Christian walk. What is even worse is, that sin and stress will fog our minds and steal away the peace that God gives us. We are to let the peace of God which passes all understanding rule in our hearts and minds,[68] not the worries and fears that come from a life of disobedience. Fear is not a gift from God; but fear is a gift from the enemy.[69] God does not give us the spirit of fear but He does give us authority, love and a sound mind. 1 Peter 5:7 continues this thought in telling us that God wants us to cast our cares and worries upon him because he loves us.

"Casting all your care upon him; for he careth for you."

This literally means that God will take care of us. He is the One to meet our needs and to bring us comfort in life. He will carry our burdens so that we do not get weighed down with worry. If we do not cast our cares upon God then

---

[68] Colossians 3:15
[69] 2 Timothy 1:7

not only are we in disobedience to the Scriptures but we are in defiance to his will for our lives. God wants to take care of us. He wants us to trust him to meet our every need. By not lifting up our requests to him, we are essentially closing the door to our heavenly Father and opening the door for the enemy to come into. Sin is a doorway for demonic oppression. The enemy will enter into a person through the temptation of sin and will begin the work constructing a stronghold. We should not give ground to the enemy through a sinful life,[70] but rather let us dedicate our life unto the Lord our God. If someone has fallen into sin, it is our responsibility to come alongside of them and help them to get their heart and lives right with God. If we call upon Emmanuel he will come and cleanse the temple of our body and mind by driving out the enemy and tearing down his strongholds.

The power of prayer can never be overstated. It is a life of prayer that blesses us. When we call upon the Father confessing our sins, He hears us and gives us cleansing.[71] Just as we eat and drink everyday, so should we be confessing our sins and inadequacies.

> "If we say that we have no sin, we deceive ourselves, and the truth is not in us. If we confess our sins, he is faithful and just to forgive us our sins, and to cleanse us from all unrighteousness. If we say that we have not sinned, we make him a liar, and his word is not in us."[72]

---

[70] Ephesians 4:27
[71] John 16:23-26
[72] 1 John 1:8-10

It is living in the truth which not only sets us free, but keeps us free. When we ask God for forgiveness, He will always be faithful, to not only forgive us of our sins but to also cleanse us from all unrighteousness. Unrighteousness is not living right before God, *amongst* men. This continual act of having a clean heart before God prevents the building of strongholds inside of us.

There are many conceptions of what a stronghold is. A stronghold is an area of your life that has been given over to the enemy. Once a stronghold has been established the person will strengthen the influence of the enemy by continuing in the particular sin or pattern of wrong living. This includes both sins of omission and commission.[73] It is just as sinful for a believer to live a life in denial of their faith, by not witnessing and standing for the faith that has been delivered unto them, as it is for them to live a life of wickedness and debauchery. Both are grievous sins that affect both the believer in Christ and all those that around them. Isaiah 59: 1-2 speaks about the effects of the stronghold.

> "Behold, the LORD'S hand is not shortened, that it cannot save; neither his ear heavy, that it cannot hear: But your iniquities have separated between you and your God, and your sins have hid his face from you, that he will not hear."

---

[73] Omission is not doing what we ought to be doing and commission is doing what we should not be doing.

The Lord is able to deliver the child who calls for help but when our sins have become iniquities,[74] they are a spiritual stronghold that has been given over to the enemy. This separates us from the power of God in our life. It is because we have turned our back on God and have turned to the habitual practice of the sin. It has become a point of idolatrous worship and will seek to control the person. One of the key identifying marks of a stronghold is the believer will feel overwhelmed by the sinful habit but also helplessness to change. They are at the mercy of the sin. It is a stronghold because it has a strong-hold on a part of the person's life. I can't tell you how many times I have heard people say; ***"I don't believe God hears my prayers, I have begged and pleaded for His help but it never comes.***

They think God has turned his back on them but in reality, it is the other way around, they have turned our back on God and chose to serve the sin over him. The judgment of God is to give you your heart's desire; he gives you over to the sin that you desire. God lets you reap what you sow, giving you over to the spirit of sin, until you repent and turn back to him, renouncing your sin and confessing your need for him.

Here is an important thing to remember: The sin habit ***does not*** separate you from the love of God, but it will separate you from the power of God to work in your life. Nothing can ever separate you from God's love.[75] He is your Father and just as the father of the prodigal son waited for his return, our Father is waiting for us to call upon him and to come back to

---

[74] Iniquities are when the sin has become a pattern or habit in the person's life
[75] Romans 8:39

him.[76] As men and woman called of God, we need to be able to recognize the strongholds of the enemy and then to see to the work of having them torn down. Our weapons are mighty and they will pull down strongholds,[77] but often the strongman must be bound before he can be cast out. Here is where the work of the Christian counselor comes in;[78] by binding the spirit's influence on the person and then confronting the lies of the enemy, the walls will come down and the captive will be set free. You see the battle is over. The victory has already been won by Christ Jesus, we simply need to claim this truth and then give God the praise for it and the walls will come down![79] This brings us back to the subject of formal gathering for worship with the church body.

Forsake not the assembling of the Saints

One great goal of the enemy is to sever your gathering for formal worship with other believers. God has called for us to come out and meet together so that we can unite in praise, worship and fellowship of Him, with the rest of the church family.[80] Earlier we looked at the example of Paul in how the enemy works to destroy the believer. Like the pack of wolves the minions of Satan will sever a lamb from the protection of the flock in order

---

[76] Luke 15:20
[77] 2 Corinthians 10:4
[78] Matthew 12:29; Mark 3:27
[79] 1 Corinthians 15:57; 1 John 5:4; Joshua 6:20
[80] Hebrews 10:24-25

to kill and devour it.[81] By driving the sheep away from the protection of the flock the enemy knows that he will have a greater opportunity and time kill and devour it.

Our Lord has established formal worship for many reasons; the main reason being that He is worthy of all glory, honor and praise.[82] As His people, it is a distinct privilege afforded to us that we can come together on a regular basis for unified worship. When the house of God honors the Lord Jesus Christ, then it is a wonderful blessing to the child of God. Friend this is such an important topic that I would like to take a moment to re-emphasize the point:

It is when we gather for worship that that we hear the preaching and teachings of God's Holy Word. It is with the rest of the church body that we meet in order to hear the preaching and teaching of the word of God from His pastor.

Worship is an act of obedience to the command of Christ where he told us to take his yoke upon us and to learn of him.[83] What an enormous blessing! When two or more are gathered together in the name of Christ, He is there in the midst with them.[84] You are not just gathering with other believers, but you are also gathering with Jesus. He is in the midst of the assembly with you. Sadly, many people simply do not understand what they lose by forsaking the assembling of the saints. It is a very serious matter to

---

[81] Acts 20:29
[82] 1 Chronicles 16:29; Psalm 29:2, 96:9; Jeremiah 7:2; Matthew 4:10; Luke 4:8
[83] Matthew 11:29
[84] Matthew 18:20

forsake the assembling of the saints of God for worship.[85] This is the sin of omission. It is when you do not do what you know is right. The Scriptures teach:

> "Therefore to him that knoweth to do good, and doeth it not, to him it is sin."[86]

We must never forget there is power in the praise of God. When God's people gather and call upon him, praising him, the powers of heaven are released. It is a tremendous act of renewal and refreshment. God has given us instruction not to put off the formal worship service in Hebrews 10: 24-25.

> "And let us consider one another to provoke unto love and to good works: Not forsaking the assembling of ourselves together, as the manner of some is; but exhorting one another: and so much the more, as ye see the day approaching."

The formal worship is not something that God needs, God is complete in himself. The worship of God is for us. When believers meet together they are strengthened by the power of God flowing through the body of Christ. We are also provoked to good works by one another. We know that we are

---

[85] Hebrews 10:25
[86] James 4:17

not alone but are part of a greater good, filled and controlled by the Holy Spirit of God. We are the body of the Lord Jesus Christ and He is our head. We find our place in the body of believer's. All of this happens when they gather together in Christ's name. It is with the rest of the church body that we find a place where we can share our burdens with one another, and then lift them up to the Father in agreement with prayer.

"Again I say unto you, That if two of you shall agree on earth as touching anything that they shall ask, it shall be done for them of my Father which is in heaven."[87]

This is a precious promise from God and God cannot lie.[88] It is in the worship service, that we are obeying the commandment of the Lord to take his yoke upon us and learn of him. God has given to the church pastors, who are the teachers of God that He uses to equip and complete the individual believers so they can corporately and individually do the work of the Lord.[89] This is not just speaking of evangelism or missions but more importantly, how to live a life, lead by the Spirit of God, in His righteousness.

 Those who do not have a regular teaching of the word of God are just like a child deprived of nourishment and affection; both of which are necessary to live and grow. It is a horrible sight to see children who have been severely neglected. I remember seeing a ten year old boy, who could

---

[87] Matthew 18:19
[88] Titus 1:2
[89] Ephesians 4:11-12

not even stand! He was still in a crib, due to the lack of proper nutrition. He had never grown physically or mentally. This is something you never forget. It is just as saddening for a pastor to have members in his care that never show up to church service to feed on the life giving word of God. These Christians never grow or develop to full spiritual maturity. God gives you the gift of a Pastor to teach you in order to make you complete for the work of God and the life of a believer. Those who are not growing in the word will constantly be questioning the word and the will of God. They will also be like the lone sheep under attack of the enemy. Not attending regular services is disobedience to the Lord Jesus Christ and the Scriptures. This habit of life will open doorways for the enemy to enter into and once the enemy enters into that doorway, he will set up a stronghold. It is from that stronghold that he will work all sorts of havoc in the person's life. If a believer does not have a driving desire to attend the worship service of the Lord, then it is a sure sign that either, the believer has grown cold in the things of the Lord or they were never truly born again. At best this is clear evidence of a stronghold!

Our enemy does not sleep nor does he rest. He is constantly at work against the Lord and His children. It is his desire to hinder the advances of God's kingdom in every way possible. If he can weaken the individual soldiers, he can hinder the entire body in their work. Sin has to be taken seriously. The Scriptures teach that a little leaven, i.e. sin, will spread to all the members of the church body.[90] Just as putting a little yeast into some flour and water will causes the entire bowl of dough to rise; one unrepentant member can affect the entire body of believers. In Joshua 7, the sin of one man named Achan caused judgment to come upon the entire nation of Israel. Just like Israel was made up of people from all the different tribes, each church is made up of individual members from all types of backgrounds and walks of life. God has given each individual member to the specific church body they are in so they can function as a cooperative group to do the work of Christ's body on earth. A simple infection or flu can sicken a person's entire body, making the most basic functions of life painful and slow, so can the actions, or lack of actions, of one individual member infect and affect the entire church body of Christ.

Not only is fellowshipping with believers important but also is studying God's word daily. God speaks to us through his word. He uses his word to show us the way in which we are to live. A strong preventive measure against sin is to memorize God's word and to hide it in our hearts.[91] God uses His word to cleanse us.[92] Our souls are purified by our obedience to God's word.[93] We are sanctified by the word of God.[94] God's word is the meat and drink of the believer. It is not only the way in which faith for

---

[90] Matthew 16:6; 1 Corinthians 5:6-9
[91] Psalm 119:11
[92] John 15:3
[93] 1 Peter 1:22
[94] John 17:17

salvation comes to us,[95] but it is also the instrument which strengthens and increases our faith.

We serve a wonderfully awesome God. He has given us everything we need in order to live life.[96] But it is our personal responsibility to grow in His knowledge and to appropriate what He has given us. I have purposely been overly redundant in this chapter to emphasize the importance of these basic life practices. The enemy will seek to destroy the child of God. He will also seek to keep the church of God from working together in expanding the Kingdom of our Lord God. There is a battle happening between the Kingdom of light and the kingdom of darkness. The children of God are like a flock of sheep in a hostile and cruel world. But we have a Shepherd that is watching over us and He does not want us to be ignorant of the schemes of the devil. In this chapter we discussed the four most common tactics that the enemy uses against God's Children:

1) He will try to separate the believer from the fellowship of other Christians
2) He will try to hinder or stop the believer from partaking in the worship service on a regular basis
3) He will try to stop the daily devotions of Bible reading of the individual
4) He will try to hinder or stop our prayer life.

---

[95] Romans 10:17
[96] 1 Peter 1:3-4

Spiritual warfare is a part of the ministry and mission of the church of Christ. Let us stand in the faith of the living Savior and in the strength of His might. If God has spoken to your heart about anything from this last chapter will you make some notes on it below and then take it to the Lord in prayer?

_____

_____

_____

_____

_____

_____

_____

_____

_____.

Praying On The Armor ...

"Finally, my brethren, be strong in the Lord, and in the power of his might. Put on the whole amour of God, that ye may be able to stand against the wiles of the devil. For we wrestle not against flesh and blood, but against principalities, against powers, against the rulers of the darkness of this world, against spiritual wickedness in high places. Wherefore take unto you the whole armor of God, that ye may be able to withstand in the evil day, and having done all, to stand."[97]

The day we became a child of God, the enemies of our Lord set themselves against us. They became our enemy. Satan went against Christ in heaven and for this he was cast down to earth. When Jesus came to earth once again the devil tried to kill him in his infancy through the hand of King Herod. The entire time Jesus was upon the earth, he was hated, rejected, despised with even his own siblings going against him. The world and the devil are enemies of the Lord Jesus Christ. We are not greater than our Master.[98] The world hated Him and it will also hate us.[99] Isaiah 59:15 states that those who seek to depart from evil make themselves a prey.

---
[97] Ephesians 6:10-13
[98] John 13:16, 15:20; Revelation 12:7; Luke 10:18; Matthew 2:13-ff.
[99] John 17:14

> "Yea, truth faileth; and he that departeth from evil maketh himself a prey: and the LORD saw it, and it displeased him that there was no judgment."

Simply put this means:

1) The World hated our Lord and sought to destroy him.
2) The world now hates us for being His children and wants to destroy us.
3) If we seek to live righteously the enemy of our Lord will set himself against us and we will suffer persecution.[100]

Our enemy travels around like a roaring lion and the prey that he is seeking to devour are the children of God.[101] That is the reason that God has provided armor for his children to wear. His armor is designed, not for us to fight in, but to protect us from the enemy. When a person seeks to depart from evil and live for the Lord Jesus Christ, the devil and all those of the world that are his children will set themselves against the child of God. There is a war between the two families; the children of God and the children of the Devil. The devil now goes about trying to instill fear in us, similar to the lion. A roar can be heard up to two miles away. When a lion roars it causes two reactions; the animals that are hiding will break out into a

---
[100] 2Timothy 3:12
[101] 1 Peter 5:8

full run in a state of panic, or they will freeze in fear unable to move. This makes them both vulnerable to the attack of the lion! The Devil is the roaring lion and his desire is to completely devour us. He doesn't just want to hurt us or maim; he wants our complete destruction. Devour is a term meaning to swallow whole. The Devil wants to consume us with fear, not so much from an internal position but more so what is suggested it to digest so you are completely inside of him as a type of prison or dark covering. Just like the great fish was not in Jonah, Jonah was in the great fish. It was a type of prison for Jonah but it was also a time of hellish torment! The Devil wants us to panic and run in a state of fear. If a person can be made to run they will wear themselves out. They will always be tired. It will weaken them physically. It will also take their minds off of what is important, those things that are needful and will place it on the problems and worry. The beauty of this is that when we are weak God is strong on our behalf.[102] Our God is near. He is a present help in time of trouble.[103] Even when we walk through the valley of the shadow of death, with all types of creatures of prey waiting to pounce from the darkness, we do not need to fear for the Lord is with us.[104]

Friends, it's not just the Devil that is against; he has an army of minions, fallen spirits that work continually to trap us or to set us up for destruction. The Bible likens the attacks of our enemy to the shooting of fiery darts at the believers. I remember growing up watching western movies

---

[102] 2 Corinthians 13:9
[103] Psalm 46:1, 75:1; Isaiah 50:8, 55:6
[104] Psalm 23

and in them they would show the Indians attacking the fort with a barrage of arrows flying everywhere. This is not the case of real life. In real life, the Indian expected to hit what he was aiming at. Actually he intended to strike a death blow every time he shot an arrow. I heard a comment from a Native American Indian, which to me was very profound. He said that when an Indian shot an arrow they expected to hear the thud, as it struck the enemy. I asked him why and he said; "Did you ever make an arrow?" It takes a long time to make a good arrow. You couldn't just go and buy a quiver full of arrows. It would take a whole day to make just a few arrows. Arrows were very valuable so when they fired an arrow; you made every shot count.

Our enemy puts a great deal of thought and work into the weapons that he uses against us. It's not a battle that is easily seen. Often an arrow was shot from a distance and the person struck never even heard it coming, let alone saw the person who shot them. My father called the bow and arrow *silent death* for this reason. The Bible tells us who our enemy is:

> "For we wrestle **not** against flesh and blood, **but against** principalities, against powers, against the rulers of the darkness of this world, against spiritual wickedness in high places."[105]

Our battle is not against flesh and blood. Our war is not against mankind. We are all descendants of Adam and Eve. We are all related to one another. The Bible clearly tells us that we are in a battle against spiritual forces; a

---

[105] Ephesians 6:12

fallen angelic world that inhabits fallen men and then pits them against one another, in an attempt to bring about their eternal destruction. If our battle was against other people, it would be easy to identify them and to ward off their attacks. Our battle is not against flesh and blood; it is against the demonic realm. Ephesians 6:12 list four types of entities that we are in a wrestling match against:[106]

    1) Principalities

    2) Powers

    3) The Rulers of Darkness of this world

    4) Spiritual Wickedness in high places

These are four types, of demonic ruling angels, which are part of an active militant opposition that is highly organized and lead by the Devil. The type of warfare that they wage is something completely different than just physical confrontation; they will use feelings, emotions, thoughts and passions against a person. The word in Ephesians 6:12 used for wrestle is *pale* and it means to try and throw the person with the desire to pin and hold them down; preferably by the neck. This is the way a lion attacks. It grabs its prey and then holds it down by the throat until its life flows out of it. The Devil and his minions desire to throw us to the ground and then to hold us down so that we cannot move. It is his desire to put into a state of fear, hopelessness and helplessness. He will use family, friends, society and the world systems against you in this struggle. This is why God has given us His

---

[106] For a detailed study on angels and demons I recommend my book, "The Beast within."

armor and then instructed us to put it on. It is for us to be able ***to withstand*** against the schemes of the devil. By donning the armor of God we can withstand the attacks of Satan and his evil minions. There are four areas that the armor of God helps us in:

1) It helps us to set ourselves against the forces of darkness
2) It makes it so we can withstand the attacks of the enemy
3) It enables us to resist the attacks of the enemy
4) It equips us to oppose the forces of darkness

God's holy armor is the armor of light; it drives back the darkness.

> "The night is far spent, the day is at hand: let us therefore cast off the works of darkness, and let us put on the ***armour of light***."[107]

I would like to take a moment to exposit this verse as it reveals the nature of the battle we are in.

The night is far spent . . .

Paul is literally telling the believers that the time of night when they are to be sleeping is over; it's time to get up and to get ready for the day. As Believers in Christ, the time to awaken is now![108]

---

[107] Romans 13:12
[108] Roman 13:11

The day is at hand . . .

Literally the day has been bought and given to you. God has delivered the day to you so that you can now do the work that is necessary; to do the work of Christ amongst mankind. A person does not have the ability to see in the middle of the night when it is completely dark. They are weary from a long day and are in need of sleep. God has given us rest and the night is over. By the power of God, who will strengthen you, you are to rise and face the new day.[109]

Therefore let us cast off the works of darkness . . .

Put off accordingly and put off consequently the business and employment of darkness, stop allowing and participating in that which blinds not only your eyes to the truth but also the eyes of those who are around you.

And let us put on the armor of light . . .

And in doing so, literally putting off the business of darkness, let us sink, like resting in a well tailored, comforting, piece of clothing, into the armor that was created just for us, tailored to our exact dimensions. This armor is designed and filled with the light of Christ so that as we wear it, the armor emitting light and driving back, the darkness that surrounds all the people that are around. We are a light to the world,

---
[109] Ephesians 6:10; Deuteronomy 3:38; Psalm 27:14; 68:28; Isaiah 41:10; 1 Peter 5:10

because Jesus, The Light of the world is within us.[110] Let us rest in being light bearers of Christ to the world.[111]

Soldiers would take their armor off at night to rest but when the morning arose they would wash and then dress in their battle gear so they were ready for the day. Before they stepped out of their quarters they were fully dressed to meet the day. Though we may not feel like we are a soldier, God tells us that we are to live out life the way a good soldier did, with discipline and focus.

"Thou therefore, my son, be strong in the grace that is in Christ Jesus. And the things that thou hast heard of me among many witnesses, the same commit thou to faithful men, who shall be able to teach others also. Thou therefore endure hardness, as a good soldier of Jesus Christ. No man that warreth entangleth himself with the affairs of this life; that he may please him who hath chosen him to be a soldier. And if a man also strive for masteries, yet is he not crowned, except he strive lawfully."[112]

Friends the battle is the Lords and we are His children. Though it may not always be apparent we are engaged in a battle for righteousness. We are to be striving to live a righteous life, that other will see our good works and glorify our Father in heaven. All we do and say should be for the purpose of bringing God glory. But friends we are also marching towards the gates of

---

[110] Matthew 5:14-16; John 8:12, 9:5
[111] Matthew 5:16
[112] 2 Timothy 2:1-5

hell, confronting the sin of this world and the helpless estates of the fallen race seeking to see others grasped from the place of death and given life in the hand of the Savior. We are to be doing the work of the holy priest of God and this means we intercede on behalf of those in need. By this I do not mean to imply that any of us are the Great Intercessor, the alone is the Lord Jesus Christ, but as his children and priests we are to be lifting them up before God the Father and beseeching Him to forgive their sins and to grant them salvation.[113]

    The Christian life is a new and fresh experience every day. God gives us a new day, every day. God makes His promises new every morning.[114] We have God's promises of protection and blessings given to us new every day. Aren't you glad that you can have a fresh start every day? Every day we make mistakes, every day we commit sins and trespasses. Praise is to God because He promises to forgive and cleanse us, every day. Aren't you glad that these blessings are yours to claim? The enemy of our Lord does not take vacations or days off; he is continually looking for ways to attack and tear us down and that is why each and every day we need to pray on the armor of God. Just as God makes each day new with a new sun rising to shine upon our faces, we as soldiers of the cross need to don the armor of God and prepare for the battle that is certainly awaiting us when we step out into the world.

---

[113] 1 Corinthians 10:31; 2 Corinthians 4:15; Philippians 2:11; 1 Peter 2:9-12
[114] Lamentation 3:22-23

The Amor is an acknowledgment of faith

We put the armor of God by acknowledge and claiming in prayer the truths that God has given us in His word. It is trusting God to do what He has said He will do. It is claiming God's promises and then resting in them. We put the armor on by acknowledging our faith in God. It settles our minds upon what God has done for us and His preserving power in us so that we can face the day in the power of his might.[115] We can this through the power of prayer. The following is a prayer that I use to pray on the armor of God. Read it through and if you like claim it as your own or preferably learn from it and begin praying as the Lord leads you. If you agree with the prayer than go ahead and pray it after you read it.

Dear heavenly Father I claim by faith the armor of God;[116] your heavenly armor. I claim it as my own this day, the armor of light as described in Romans 13:12. I ask you to place strongly upon my head the helmet of salvation, this day O'Lord to protect my mind from the attacks of the enemy. Lord Jesus you are my covering, You are my hope and my salvation please help me this day to take all my thoughts captive and to bring them into submission under Your authority for you are my Lord and my God. Please protect my mind from the enticements that may seek to lead me astray. Help me to keep from eyes from gazing upon unholy things and my brain and mind from having unholy thoughts. I want to be pleasing to you

---
[115] Ephesians 6:10
[116] Ephesians 6:11

this day, my Holy Sovereign. I trust in your Sovereign Holy power and the helmet you have given me to keep me from harm's way. Keep me strong in the assurance of thy salvation and the trusting in your promises. So often times I am plagued with doubts but I know what time these come upon me I can trust in You. Please protect my thoughts, O'God my Father and keep my mind through Christ Jesus. I thank you heavenly Father that you will not only be my covering this day but you will watch over me as the Shepherd and Bishop of my soul.[117] You will protect my mind, brain and all my thought processes, with Your helmet of salvation. I can trust in You and rest in Your providential care, in Christ Jesus name I pray this.

Next Heavenly Father I pray that you would place upon me the girdle of truth. Lord Jesus Christ you are the Truth it by your holy blood that you have set me free and it is in your truth that I am kept free. Help me this day to experience the freedom and fullness of life that come from being in your truth. Father you have said that all liars will have their place in the lake of fire and that those that lie are of the father the devil. This is an abomination unto you and against you as you are the Truth.[118] I renounce the lies of the devil this day and ask that you would fill me with your truth. I want to honor you with all that I say and do. Let the words of my mouth be few and let them be the speech of heaven where you are continually praised and adored. Let my mouth honor you in everything I say. Let my conversation glorify you in every way. Father this day I pray and ask that you wrap me in your

---

[117] 1 Peter 2:25
[118] Revelations 21:8; Proverbs 6:17; John 8:44

holy armor. Girt my loins with your truth and let me be a shining example of the Lord Jesus Christ to the world today. Help me to do this O'Lord as I can do nothing on my own. I trust in you, for you are my God and King.

    Lord, God next I pray and ask that you would place upon me the breastplate of righteousness. Lord Jesus you alone are the holy sinless only begotten of the Father, you have imputed unto me your righteousness and have taken my sins. I give you my praise and glorify your name in the great word you have done for me. I pray this day that you would take control of my heart, my bowels and use them for your purpose and will this day O'Lord. These are the seats of my will and emotions. I pray that you would be God over my will and emotions and that Your throne would be firmly established over my heart this day. Rule over all that I am, be the Lord of my life. Let me not turn aside from your righteousness. Keep my mind and heart upon you, this day. Let me not be turned aside by unruly passions but rather let my heart and mind be stayed upon you Christ Jesus my Lord. I pray that others would see the righteousness of Christ in me and through me this day heavenly Father. I pray as I go out into the world today and also in the confines of my home that the righteousness of Christ would radiate in me and through me. Let the entire world know of my righteous King, Who is God over all creation. Lord Convict me this day of my sins. I am human and in this body of flesh. I do not want to, but Lord I know my weakness. I pray you would convict me of sin, righteousness and judgment this day so that I may have a clean heart; one that is wholly set apart for you. Lead me not into transgression but deliver me from all evil and the evil one this day. Let all that is within me this day praise you, my Lord and my God.

Father I also pray that you would wrap my feat in the shoes of the gospel of peace. Lord you bless the peace makers, they are your children. Father I am your child let me be characterized by you as one that seeks to bring peace to those in the world.[119] I want to see others in Christ this day heavenly Father. I pray that you would use me in the ministry of reconciliation.[120] Father let me love others as you loved me. Let me seek to be a peace maker to bring honor unto your name. Lord, I want to see others committing their lives to you and desiring to live for you. Lord only you can give salvation for salvation is of You, O' Lord. You have commanded all of your children to go out and to give the gospel to all we meet, to invite them to the great Marriage feast of the Lamb, to plead with them to turn from the world and unto you for salvation;[121] making them disciples and seeing them baptized in Your Name Father and of the Son, the Lord Jesus Christ and of the Holy Spirit.[122] Lord prepare my feet this day with the gospel of peace that I may live and tell others of the good news in Jesus Christ.

Finally Lord I pray that your shield of faith would be all around me. Shield me from all the fiery darts of the enemy. Lord faith is committing unto you, I pray that you would help me this day to be committed to

---

[119] Matthew 5:9
[120] 2 Corinthians 5:18-19
[121] Luke 14:23, Matthew 24:14, 28:18-20; Mark 1:14, 8:35; Acts 14:7; Romans 1:16, 10:15
[122] Jonah 2:9; Genesis 49:18; Exodus 15:2; Deuteronomy 32:15; 1 Samuel 2:1; 2 Samuel 22:3, 47; 1 Chronicles 16:23; 2 Chronicles 6:4; Job 13:16; Psalm 3:8, 13:5, 18:2, 46, 20:5, 25:5; 27:1, 37:9, 50:23; Isaiah 12:2-3, 52:7, 59:17, 61:10; Acts 4:12, 13:26

everything about you; your word, your will and your place over all of my life. This day I will trust in you to keep me committed unto you for we are kept by your power to the end of our salvation.[123] Lord this day I also take up the sword of the spirit, which is your holy word. I pray that you will enable me to study to show myself approved unto you, a workman that needeth not to be ashamed but help me to rightly divide the word of truth from error. Lord, direct my conversation that it will be seasoned with your holy word making others hungry for righteousness. Use my tongue to edify others as you direct. And Lord, help me to always say those things that become the gospel of the Lord Jesus Christ. Father I know your sword is sharper than any two edged sword and that it can cut to the heart of a person, dividing the soul and spirit but I pray that Father as I use you word it would not be in a way that causes others to reject you but rather let me handle the word skillfully so that others come to a right understanding of you in Christ Jesus. I pray that today I would be equipped with your complete armor, the armor of light and that I would stand in this evil day and would see your mighty hand reach out and touch all those around me. Let me see your mighty works this day, in Christ's name I do pray, Amen.

When you pray on the armor, don't let it become an empty ritual. It's not simply memorizing a set of words and repeating them, like a chant or mantra. It is acknowledging the power of God in your life. Do not let what the Lord has done for you and what he is going to do for you, ever lose it value and meaning in your life. Keep your relationship fresh and strong.

---

[123] 1 Peter 1:5

Take time to remember where you where and from where you came. Think of the day of your salvation and how everything in your life changed.[124] If you truly are in Christ everything has changed.[125] When we pray unto God it must be heartfelt and honest. Keep your prayer life fresh and personal. Come to the Lord in faith, believing that He is, and that He is a re-warder of those who diligently seek him.[126] Tell God you are placing this armor on by faith. Understanding the components of the armor and applying them to your life is a serious matter when you are engaged in spiritual warfare. Let me explain why.

Early in my ministry, I entered into a counseling session without praying on the armor of God. The young man that I was to counsel seemed like a rather a nice fellow and I had seen nothing to indicate that I was going to be involved, in spiritual warfare during this session. The previous Sunday he had came forward to receive salvation and wanted to meet with me to discuss joining the church. I explained that since he had just received salvation that his next step was to follow the Lord in believer's baptism. The churches policy was that by being baptized before the church he would automatically become a member of our congregation. He told me he did not want to be baptized; he just wanted to be a member. What I did not know about him, but found out later was that he had formerly been involved in

---

[124] Revelations 3:#
[125] You are a new creation in Christ Jesus. 2 Corinthians 5:17
[126] Hebrews 11:6

Satanism. Actually he was a multi-generationalist.[127] I asked the young man to come to my office to discuss what biblical baptism was and what the church's position also was on membership. As we settled into our seats, I had no sooner prayed for the Lords blessing on our discussion, when I came under an incredible demonic attack. A spirit physically grabbed my head and lifted me out of my chair, shaking me violently in the air. It felt like my head was being crushed. I was not even able to cry out as my mouth was being held by whatever was crushing my head. Out of the corner of my eye, I could see my prayer partner was also lifted out of his seat and being shaken violently. I cried out in my mind for God to help me and instantly whatever it was that had been holding me let go dropping me into my chair. I then cried out to God for my prayer partner and it let him go. The young man was now completely possessed by the demonic spirit and calmly said to me, "*I don't have to touch you, to hurt you. I'm going to leave now.*" He calmly got up and walked out of my office. I had never suspected this man to be a former occultist but when I prayed it triggered a strong reaction from the enemy. Sadly, this young man never returned to church but went back to his satanic family. I believe the man may have been sent to infiltrate the church in order to work from the inside to try and destroy the fellowship of the church. I have heard from several former Satanists that they were sent into the church in order to curse the members and to destroy the churches outreach to the community.

---

[127] A multi-generationalist is someone whose family line has been involved in that particular religion for several generations. In this case the family religion for several hundred years had been Satanism.

Though this was a good learning experience it also was heart breaking. The man who was with me in the session was a young believer in Christ and he ended up quitting and leaving the church with his family over this. He could not get over what had happened in the office. I learned a very painful lesson that day about not being serious when praying on the armor of God and in praying for the Lord to bind any evil influence in the office. Anytime I have a meeting with someone now, I come before the Lord and claim His promises, praying on the armor. I do this before any counseling session, no matter how innocent the person may appear to be.

Let me take a few moments to recap what was said before. I always begin with the helmet of salvation then I ask the Lord to place upon me the breastplate of righteousness. This is to enable me to live righteously, that day before God and amongst men. I then ask the Lord to protect all of my inner bowels and emotions with the breastplate and to surround me with the righteousness of Jesus Christ. This is extremely important. While counseling people wanting to come out of the occult I have literally come under such demonic attack, that I felt like I was having a severe heart attack. The breastplate of righteousness will protect your inner organs and emotions. Following the breastplate, ask the Lord to place the belt of truth upon you, keeping you in the truth of Jesus Christ. As Jesus is the Truth ask Him to wrap you in His truth and to keep you free. Before you finish praying, take the time to pray for friends and enemies alike. Ask God to bless them and to change them according to His perfect will. Pray for all their needs and however the Lord leads you by His Spirit. Spiritual warfare is all around the believer. The battle is already there waiting for you each day so begin the day by preparing yourself and then resting in God's holy armor.

Spiritual Warfare is a part of the Priesthood

Spiritual Warfare is the job, of the priest of God. The spiritual realm is the arena of the priest of God. God has made us warrior Priests. We are to stand watch, for not only ourselves, but the church of God and those that God brings to us for counseling.[128] Jesus Christ as our Commander and Chief wears a different piece of armor than we, who are his bride. Christ's armor is described as also containing the cloak of vengeance.[129] Vengeance belongs to God only. We are to have mercy, love and compassion on those we work with. The weapons of our warfare are not carnal or fleshly but they do have the ability to tear down strongholds of the enemy.[130] Remember those who are living lives in disobedience and sometimes open defiance against the Lord Jesus Christ are not our enemies; they are being used by the enemy! Many people are enslaved by the enemy because they have believed lies from the enemy. That is why it is by experiencing the truth of God that they are set free.[131] Another thing we should understand about spiritual warfare is that the battle is not ours; it is the Lord's. Any battle that we face will not be won by power nor might that the battle can only be won through

---

[128] Jeremiah 6:17, 31:6; Isaiah 62:6
[129] Isaiah 59
[130] 2 Corinthians 10:3-7
[131] John 8:32, 14:6

the Holy Spirit of God.[132] If we seek to do anything in our flesh, we will be defeated. By standing clothed in God's armor and calling upon the Lord Jesus Christ the victory will come.[133] As the Leader of the armies of heaven, when Christ goes into battle; He goes forth to win. All creation, everything in heaven and upon earth bow at His feet. As His bride, He will protect us no matter what we encounter.

Whenever I encounter a stubborn demonic stronghold in counseling, I have found that by commanding the entity to state, out loud, through the person's mouth, that Jesus Christ is King of kings and Lord of lords. They have to honor him and they have to obey his servant. All angels are ministering spirits to those who are heirs to salvation, this means they have to obey a born again child of God.[134] Next, I command them to speak truth that will stand before the Lord Jesus Christ on the Day of Judgment, when he judges them at his great white throne and affirm if I am a true child of God. When they answer yes, I make them openly confess that since I am a child of God they have to obey me. This does two things:

1) It breaks the power of obstinate entities over the person
2) It gives hope and strength to the person the entity is in

I will next ask the entity if the person I am counseling is truly a born again child of God? If they answer yes, I then make them state that they also have

---

[132] Zechariah 4:6
[133] Psalm 50:15, 91:15, Jeremiah 29:12
[134] Hebrews 1:14

to obey them; and they do. If they say the person is not a child of God, I then take the time to ask the person to tell me about their salvation experience. I then take the time to teach them on what the Bible teaches on salvation. If they agree with the Scriptures then ask the person if they would like to pray and receive the Lord Jesus Christ as their personal Savior. The Bible is very clear; all angels whether good or bad are servants to God's children. They have to obey the child of God as long as the request is according to his revealed will.[135] The Bible also tells us in Colossians 2:13-15 that all the fallen angels/demons have been defeated and that they know who the children of God are.

> "And you, being dead in your sins and the uncircumcision of your flesh, hath he quickened together with him, having forgiven you all trespasses; Blotting out the handwriting of ordinances that was against us, which was contrary to us, and took it out of the way, nailing it to his cross; And having spoiled principalities and powers, he made a shew of them openly, triumphing over them in it."

After we have established that the person is a child of God's, I again will make the entity say loudly, (as they often try to just whisper it), that Jesus Christ is King of kings and Lord of lords, and that they have to bow the knee to him, which they do. You see the Bible is very clear, at the name of Jesus, every knee must bow and every tongue confess that Jesus is

---

[135] Hebrew 1:14; James 4:3

Lord.[136] This weakens the hold that they have on the individual. Many times the person does not know why they have the demonic stronghold. A demonic stronghold is the result of either perpetual sin, a curse upon the individual or by believing and embracing a lie from the devil. In order to confront the lies of the devil you will need to know the truth of God's word.

Being battle ready is not only important; it can save your life. Talk to any veteran about protective armor and they will be able to give you real life examples in how many lives that have been saved by a helmet or vest. Those who seek to live righteously for Christ will be a prey. Put on the whole armor of God so you can stand in the day.

In summation the armor God, is the armor of light. When we don the helmet of salvation, it not only protects our thoughts but puts them on the good things of God, so that we can tell others of the grace and salvation of our Great and High God. When we put on the breastplate of righteousness it protects our emotions and keeps them safe from the enemy's touch and manipulation. The belt of truth keeps us in the truth by surrounding us with the truth. The shoes of peace enable us to be the peace makers of God. The shield of faith is our commitment to God and the sword of the spirit which is the word of God, complete the armor of the light. This armor drives back the darkness surrounding those we meet. It allows the light of Christ to shine through us into this world of darkness, lighting the way for others to see the pathway of life and to embrace the saving faith of Jesus Christ.

---

[136] Philippians 2:10

Generational Curses ...

AHHHH! The man screamed out as he threw himself backwards. Both chair and man flew backwards from the table. It all happened so fast that it seemed unreal. I sat looking at a forty seven year old man with his arms tightly wrapped around himself, like a small child. His whole body was shaking and spasming from head to toe, as if he was freezing to death. He had this look of terror in his eyes. I calmly asked; "Are you having a little trouble praying the prayer?"

Earlier this man had come to see me if he could discover the reason why his whole life was nothing but repeated failures. I suspected that he may be suffering from a curse so I set a prayer before him to renounce curses. After praying the first sentence, he screamed and threw himself backwards shaking and jerking uncontrollably. "I, I can't pray that! I CAN'T PRAY THAT!" he screamed. With that he jumped up and ran out of the building before I could stop him. This man was suffering from what is properly termed, *"a generational curse."* Generational curses have incredible power to do evil, just as generational blessings have wonderful power for good. We read of the legality of the generational curse in the book of Exodus.

"And the LORD descended in the cloud, and stood with him there, and proclaimed the name of the LORD. And the LORD passed by before him, and proclaimed, The LORD, The LORD God, merciful and gracious, longsuffering, and abundant in goodness and truth, Keeping mercy for thousands, forgiving iniquity and transgression and sin, and that ***will by no means clear the guilty; visiting the iniquity*** of the fathers upon the children, and upon the children's children, unto the third and to the fourth generation."[137]

Our Lord is very gracious and merciful to all those who call upon him, but those who do not repent and renounce their sins, leave an opened doorway, for their iniquities to be visited upon their children and their children's all children, all the way to the third and fourth generation. This creates a never ending cycle of sin, with the effects of the sin, which is the curse, continually affecting the children of the family line and being passed to their children, their grandchildren and great grandchildren. This perpetual curse of sin will continue to be passed into each successive generation until the sin is confessed and renounced by one of the victims. The man described above was a very pleasant, likable individual. He was good natured and actually very enjoyable to be around. He had been a born again believer for several decades. He came to me because his entire life and that of his siblings could only be described as one of poverty and great loss. None of them could get ahead no matter how hard they tried. In this man's case every business venture that he would start would end by an unexpected calamity. No matter how hard he tried, no matter what he tried; he could not get on his feet. Every good job he had would either be lost through accident, injury or cut

---

[137] Exodus 34:5-7

backs and now at forty seven he had nowhere to live, no vehicle and no money. He had been married and divorced several times. His last wife had a home that was paid for, several cars and a great deal of money in the bank until she married him. They were hit with unexpected catastrophes; one right after another until they went broke. His wife ended up losing her home, which had been paid for prior to marriage and all of her possessions. She lost a good job that she had been in for over twenty years before filing for bankruptcy and then for divorce. This man had personally owned three houses in the past but was unable to keep them. He had started several successful businesses but had lost them all through unfortunate circumstances and just plain bad luck. In discussing the topic of his life he pointed out that his father and his grandfather and everyone in their family were just haunted with bad luck. He was right. If anything could go wrong with this fellow it did. I suspected that he was suffering from a generational curse so I put a simple prayer in front of him and that was when the enemy revealed himself and his stronghold. Below is a copy of the prayer I placed in front of him. I was given this prayer by a counselor from the International School of Biblical Counselors, located in Indianapolis Indiana. (To my knowledge the school no longer exists.)

BREAKING CURSES PRAYER

Father in the name of Jesus Christ, I come to You, sincerely with a desire to be free from all curses and their results. Lord Jesus, I thank You for saving me and cleansing away my sin at the cross. I confess with my mouth that I belong to You. The devil has no power over me because I am cleansed and covered by Your precious blood. I now confess all of my sins, known and unknown. I repent of them now in the name of Jesus. I ask You, Lord to forgive me. I now confess the sins of all my forefathers. In the name and by the blood of Jesus Christ, I break and renounce the power of every demonic curse that was passed down to me through the sins and actions of others. In the name of Jesus Christ, I break the power and the hold of every curse that came to me through sin, my sins and the sins of my forefathers.

In the name of Jesus Christ, I break the power of every curse that came to me through words spoken. In the name of Jesus Christ, I break the power and hold of every curse that came to me through disobedience, mine or my forefathers.

In the name of Jesus Christ, I now renounce , break , and loose myself and my family from all demonic subjection, to my father, mother, grandparents or any other human being, living or dead, who has ever in the past or are now dominating or controlling me or my family in any way contrary to the Word and will of God.

In the name of Jesus Chris, I renounce, break, and loose myself and my family from all psychic heredity, demonic strongholds, psychic power, bondages, bonds of inherited physical or mental illness or curses upon me and my family line as a result of sins, transgressions, iniquities occult, or psychic involvement of any member of my family line, living or dead.

In the name of Jesus Christ, I declare every legal hold and every legal ground of the enemy broken and destroyed. Satan no longer has a legal right to harass my family line through curses. Through the blood of Jesus Christ, I am free. Thank You, Jesus, for setting me free.

In the name of Jesus Christ, I command all demonic spirits that entered me through curses to leave me now. Go! In the name of Jesus! I confess that my body, soul, and spirit is the dwelling place of the Spirit of God. I am redeemed, cleansed, sanctified, and justified by the blood of Jesus. Therefore neither Satan nor his demons have any place in me, nor power over me because of Jesus. THANK YOU JESUS FOR SETTING ME FREE![138]

Generational curses can be removed

Several weeks later the man returned to my office wanting to know why he could not pray the prayer on curses. I had been praying for God to bring him back so I could try and help him. Before I started the session with him, I asked if he would give me permission to pray on his behalf, in proxy with authority. **Now this is a very important lesson to learn.** A Child of God can pray on behalf and in place of another person if they give them permission. This is called praying for them, via proxy with authority. He gave me permission so I asked the Lord to seal the office and to bind all

---

[138] International School for Biblical Counseling ; Spiritual Warfare Course I, ISBC, Sioux City, Iowa

spirits, including the spirits of earth, air wind, water, nature, metal, wood and spirit itself, severing all interaction between them and bringing them under the authority of Christ. I next asked the Lord to bind the principalities, power's, dominion's, rulers of darkness of this present age and all spiritual wickedness in high places and then to release the power of the Holy Spirit of love, power and a sound mind. At this point in the prayer, I asked the Lord to come into the persons mind and to bring order to the chaotic, autonomic structure of his body, mind, soul and spirit. I then asked the Lord to bind anything that would hinder him from hearing the voice of the Lord. I then asked the Lord to speak to his mind and to reveal to him, if he was truly a child of God; he said the Lord told him yes. I then asked the Lord why he could not pray the prayer; he looked up from prayer and said the Lord told him he was under a generational curse. He said the Lord revealed to him that a curse had been placed on his family line, by a man that his ancestor had cheated out of a home and land. In anger this man had cursed his great grandfather and his children forever so that they would all suffer the same loss of their homes and property and that they would be forever in poverty. I asked the Lord, what the man needed to do in order to get rid of the curse and he said the Lord told him to confess the sin of his ancestor and to then renounce the curse.

Here is how I lead him to pray:

"Heavenly Father, I confess the dishonesty and sins of my forefathers, known and unknown, on both sides of my family lines and ask you to forgive me and my relatives, on both my mother and father's side to the thousandth generation and beyond. Forgive us for the pain that we have caused others, specifically this family that my forefather cheated and stole from. I renounce all curses associated with my family lines and ask you to take the sword of the Holy Spirit severing all unholy ties and attachments, freeing our family from this curse, casting out all demons associated with it, sending them where you command, by the voice of your Holy Spirit. Father would you please cleanse me in the blood of the Lord Jesus Christ, sealing me with your Holy Spirit and filling me in all my empty spaces with the fruit of your Holy Spirit. I thank you for your deliverance and I praise you as my God. In Jesus Christ's name I pray, Amen."

Immediately this man's' life changed, within a month he got a good job and was able to purchase a car as well as a place to live. At the time of this writing, he has had security and financial freedom for over two years. One act by his great grandfather had literally brought misery and ruin to this family line for over 100 years. The curse of sin is certainly transferable to the descendants of a person. Since the days of Adam all mankind has been under the curse of sin. The Bible teaches in Romans 5:12:

"Wherefore, as by one man sin entered into the world, and death by sin; and so death passed upon all men, for that all have sinned."

This is a clear example how the actions of one person, in this case Adam, can affect all those who will come after him. It took the holy, righteous blood of Jesus being shed on our behalf to cleanse us from the curse of sin. It is only through the shed blood of Jesus Christ that a person can be cleansed and set free from the curse of death but also given the blessing of eternal life.

False religion can be the source of generational curse

The religion of a person's ancestors can affect them and their children for many generations. I have worked with countless individuals whose ancestors had made vows to false gods in various religions such as the following:
1) Mayan
2) Celtic, Keltic or Duidic
3) German
4) The Masonic lodge or Eastern Star any other false gods
5) Witchcraft
6) Satanism
7) Lucifarianism, Deism or Elitism

The vows that have made by a father and mother have a direct impact upon their children and their children's children often causing incredible hardships or bondages that can last for centuries until confessed and renounced. The effects of these sins are reproduced generation after generation. The sin could be something as simple as idolatry, gossip or drunkenness or it may be something as severe as prostitution, murder or child molestation.

NOTE: *A Vow made to a false god is the sin of idolatry!*

Vows made to false gods have incredible power to influence the family line for generations that follow. I have personally spoken to children whose parents bring them to me because the child is seeing entities, such as black hovering spirits with glowing eyes over their beds at night, only to learn that it was a familiar spirit. Worship of demonic spirits, will create familiar ties between the evil spirit and the family line that can last for several centuries. I had a particular case where the spirit was appearing at the foot of the child's bed at night when he would try to go to sleep. The spirit was trying to enter the child through a doorway created by fear. It is not just a coincidence that many people feel attracted to occultism, with its practices or studies. This includes the martial arts. There are many types of familiar spirits the thing they all have in common is that they seek to enter into the person they appear to; usually it is a child. After they enter into a person they will gradually begin influencing the person until their thoughts are literally one. The goal of these spirits is to seek to control the person. They want to consume them.

When a person is suffering from a generational curse that involves a familiar spirit, you will need to lead them in a prayer of confession and renouncing of the specific sins that allowed the spirit to attach to the family line and also the sins that allowed the spirit to enter into the person.[139] If you do not know what that sin is then pray and ask the Lord to reveal to the person what the sin is. God will reveal what the person needs to pray to receive forgiveness and cleansing. Then lead them in prayer, asking the Lord to take the sword of the Holy Spirit and to sever all the unholy ties and attachments to the spirit and the sin. Next have them ask the Lord to wash them clean in the holy blood of Christ sending all of the spirits associated with the generational curse to where the Lord commands by the voice of His Holy Spirit. Ask him to send away from their family line and to give them a blessing in the area that was once cursed. For example; If they had a curse of alcoholism than ask the Lord to bless all of the family and their descendants with sober minds and hearts and a reliance upon the Holy Spirit of God and a repulsion to being controlled by alcohol or any other drug. Then thank the Lord for what he is going to do in their life. Finally ask the Lord to seal them in the Holy Spirit and to fill them, in all their empty spaces and voids with the fruit of the Holy Spirit. Here is an outline of the prayer:

1) Pray and ask the Lord to reveal what the sin is
2) Pray and ask for forgiveness for the sin; both for themselves and all their family line
3) Pray and ask God to take and sever them from the curse and its effect with the sword of the Holy Spirit. Also ask the Lord to sever

---

[139] 2 Corinthians 4:2

the person and all their family members from all un-holy ties and attachments

4) Pray and ask the Lord to command the spirits to go where He wills by the voice of His Holy Spirit

5) The pray and ask the Lord to fill them in all of their empty spaces and voids with the fruit of the Holy Spirit

Generational curses are just one of many different types of curses listed in the Bible. I have written a book that deals with all the curses and their effects as revealed in the Bible which I recommend if you are interested in further research.[140] Curses come in a variety of forms and can be any of the following:

1) A generational curse[141]
2) The curse of the law[142]
3) Having a curse cast on you by someone[143]
4) Touching or owning a cursed object[144]
5) Doing a cursed act [like cursing a Jewish person][145]
6) Having a idol[146]

---

[140] "Everything you always wanted to know about curses but were too afraid to ask;" by Dr. Tom Knotts, Jr.
[141] Exodus 20:5; 34:7; Numbers 14:8; Deuteronomy 5:9
[142] Galatians 3:10, 5:4
[143] Genesis 9:25
[144] Deuteronomy 7:26
[145] Genesis 27:29; Numbers 24:9; Deuteronomy 27:17

7) Disrespecting your parents[147]
8) Committing Incest[148]
9) See Deuteronomy 27 for a more complete list of curses

The bible infers that a curse is the result of someone releasing negative spiritual energy toward another person, object, or a place that is being cursed. There are 168 verses in the Scriptures, where the words curse, cursed and curses are mentioned. Deuteronomy chapters 27 and 28 give detailed descriptions of the various reasons why people are subject to a curse or being cursed.

The following are symptoms that may indicate a curse:[149]

1. A mental or emotional breakdown (Deut. 28:20, 28, 34, 65)
2. Repeated or chronic sickness, especially if it is hereditary or without clear medical diagnosis (Deut. 28:21-61)
3. Repeated miscarriages or related female problems or barrenness (Deut. 28:18) Druids and witches specialize in this type of curse as they are related to the fertility goddess
4. Marriage breakdown or family alienation in general (Deut. 28:41) Satan's desire is to destroy the family unit

---
[146] Deuteronomy 27:15
[147] Deuteronomy 27:16
[148] Deuteronomy 27:22
[149] For a detailed reading on curses I have written the book; "Everything you always wanted to know about curses but were too afraid to ask."

5. Continuing financial insufficiency, especially where the income appears sufficient. (Deut. 28: 17, 29, 47, 48; Isaiah 24:6) The devourer is a entity that's purpose is this curse

6. Being accident prone (Deut. 28:29)

7. A history of suicides or unnatural deaths in the family (Deut. 28: 21-22, 25)

Curses can come from a multitude of sources to include the prayers of other Christians. The great Christian author, Watchman Nee wrote on how we can curse other believers through our prayers. There is truth in this. The Bible tells us that from the same mouth can come forth curses and blessings, but this should not be.[150] We are to bless and curse not. Curses have limitations.The Scriptures are very clear that a curse cannot come upon a person without a cause.[151] The following are possible sources for curses:

1. Idolatry, false gods, the occult (Ex. 20:3-6; I Sam. 15:23, 24; Deut. 18:10; Acts 19:18-19)

2. Dishonoring parents (Deut.27:16; Eph. 6:1-3)

3. Illicit or unnatural sex (Lev. 18:22; Deut. 27:15-16, 20-23)

---

[150] James 3:10
[151] Proverbs 26:2

4. Injustice to the weak or helpless. The Greatest incidence of this in our society is abortion. (Deut. 27:19 & 25; Ps. 6:17)

5. Trusting in the flesh. (Jer. 17:5, 6; Gal.3:3)

6. Stealing, perjury (Zech. 5:1-4)

7. Being stingy with God financially. (Malachi 1:14, 3: 8-11)

8. Words spoken by those with relational authority (I.e. Parents, husbands, teachers, pastors) (Gen. 31:32, 35:16-19)

9. Curses people pronounce on themselves. (Gen. 27:12, 13, 46; Mark 16:7; Jn. 21: 15-17; Matt. 27:20-26)

10. Words pronounced by persons representing Satan (witchdoctors, wizards, cultists, Masons, Eastern Star members, various religious sects, etc.) (Deut. 18:10-12 ; Num. 22-24; I Cor. 10:8; 2 Pet.. 2:15-16; Jude 1 ; Rev. 2:14)

11. Fleshly prayers, words spoken with a hateful attitude, gossip. (James 3:14-15 Jer.18:18; Jude 16-19; Titus 3:2)

12. Covenants forbidden in Scripture i.e. covenants with people aligned with Satan. (Ex. 23:32)

If you believe you are under a curse the following are steps you can take to remove it. For a more in-depth set of prayers please refer to my book, "The Little Book of Prayers."

1. Confess your faith in Christ and in His sacrifice on your behalf. Rom. 10:9-10

2. Repent of all your rebellion and sin. Acts 20:21; I Sam. 15:22-23; I Jn. 1: 9

3. Submit yourself to God and resist the devil. Rom. 12:1-2; James 4:7-10

4. Remove and burn all cultic, idolatrous or satanic material (Acts 19:19)

5. Pray and ask God to reveal if you are under a curse. If you believe that you are, then pray and ask God to cancel the curse and to release you, your immediate family, and your future generations from the curse.

Many believers fall under the curse of the law

Another type of curse that can affect a believer is the curse of the law. This is where individuals cannot experience, the fullness of what it means to be accepted and loved by the Father. They live their life with a continual belief that they have to live by the law in order to please the Father. This is the curse of the law. We are saved by the grace of God it is not by our own works. If we could save ourselves by our own works than the death of Christ would have been in vain. Furthermore we did not receive salvation by keeping the law and we are not kept saved by keeping the law. The law was nothing but a schoolmaster that was to make us realize that we could not keep the law. We are sinful and condemned as a result of it. But praise be to God that we are saved by grace and kept by the power of God.[152] Some Christians believe that a person cannot curse them but I have personally witnessed the effects of individuals and their abilities to curse.

> "For as many as are of the works of the law are under the curse: for it is written, Cursed is every one that continueth not in all things which are written in the book of the law to do them."[153]

One common characteristic of those that try to live by the law is that they do not show grace or mercy to others. They tend to be hard spirited and often get angry, when others question their doctrine or ways. They also tend to be

---
[152] Ephesians 2:8-9; 1 Peter 1:5; Galatians 2:16-17, 20-21, 3:1-3, 10-13; 3:24-25
[153] Galatians 3:10: Those that try to live by the law bring a curse upon themselves.

very judgmental towards others, often exhibiting very critical spirits. They seek to live by the law and then try to recruit others into their legalistic ways of life. They are like the Pharisee, that was void of the love of God; he lived according to the law.[154] You are not saved by the law and you certainly are not kept saved, after salvation, by keeping the law. Life under the law is a curse.

A person can be cursed through direct contact with something evil

I was asked to do a wedding for a middle aged couple several years ago. The bride came to my office to set up the arrangements for the wedding. Immediately upon sitting down she stated that I had a huge aura emanating from my body. I asked her if she could see it and she said that indeed she could and that she had many spiritual gifts such as divination, palm reading, etc. She informed me that she came from a long line of Mayan priests and priestesses. I confronted her on this as being the sin of witchcraft and not a gift from the true God. Several hours later she left my office having received Jesus Christ as her personal Lord and Savior. During the process, I led her in prayers of renouncing and confessing her false worship and cultic practices and then asking the Lord Jesus to send the demons where he commanded them to go, by the voice of His Holy Spirit.

The wedding took place outdoors on the eve of the summer solstice.[155] Her family had chosen the date for the wedding and had planned on having a

---

[154] Matthew 23:15
[155] The summer solstice is one of the two most holy days to hose in the occult.

Mayan priest and priestess flown in from Southern Mexico to perform he ceremony. I had met the groom and witnessed to him a few months before the wedding and he decided that he wanted a Christian wedding instead of a Mayan service. I did not know anything about how upset the family was until after the ceremony. After I finished the wedding ceremony, I released everyone to go to the reception area. After the last persons started to leave and I was beginning to walk towards the exit, up walks the Mayan Priest and his priestess to me. He and she were dressed in all of their worship garments. I did not know who they were. As they walked up to me, the man said something I did not understand and then took his hand and ran his fingers up my shirt in a brushing manner which ending in him touching my face as he said some more words I did not understand. What he had done was to pronounce a curse upon me. Instantly I was flooded with fear. What was worse was the fact that I could see evil spirits manifesting all around me. I excused myself and, instead of going home I went to my office and called an associate to bind and pray with me to get rid of this curse. Because the Mayan priest did not get to do the ceremony, the family of the bride was very upset and had the Mayan priest curse me. The reason I performed the wedding was because the husband had insisted that I perform the wedding, telling the woman that if she wanted to get married she would have to come and discuss having me do the ceremony. After receiving the Lord she also refused to have the Mayan ceremony. This angered the family and the priest and priestess so he cursed me with death. Praise be that God the Holy Spirit that is within me is more powerful than anything of this world.[156] The only thing they accomplished was to cause me some fear and confusion for a few hours. With the help of a Christian friend, God delivered me from the curse. To sum up this chapter let me say; Curses are very real and often can be the source of a wide variety of problems. God can remove the curse and will bless the individual once the sin and the curse are renounced. God will cleanse the individual and their family line.[157]

---

[156] 1 John 4:4
[157] 2 Corinthians 4:2

Unholy ties and attachments . . .

"Pastor I just can't get him out of my head, I've prayed and prayed and tried everything, but I just can't quite thinking about him!" As she sat there looking down it was obvious that this obsessive thought was wearing her down and that she could not take much more of the harassment. The constant barrages of lustful thoughts were affecting her so severally that she was unable to do the job she had worked for over twenty years. It was also affecting her relationship with her husband, as she told me, "when I'm with my husband I can't stop thinking of the other man." This is why she had come to see me. What was happening was she was continually thinking of this other man. She was lusting after him constantly, dreaming of him at night and daydreaming about him during the day. Her problem was that she had an unholy tie; ***a soul tie.***[158]

An unholy tie or attachment is when we have a bond with someone, something, a practice, or an event, that goes against the word of God. The afore mentioned woman had broken God's word by committing adultery with a male friend from work. Even though it was a onetime event the consequence were long lasting and mentally destructive. Today the sin of adultery seems quite mild and is actually becoming a widely accepted practice. People will say, "what's the big deal? So you made a mistake just get over it." The problem was that she could not get over it! She loved her

---
[158] 1 Corinthians 6:16

husband and children but found that every waking moment, even while sleeping, she was obsessively thinking about this other man. The obsessive compulsive thought process had grown so bad that she had even called her husband by the other man's name while they were making love. What she did not know was that two weeks prior her husband had came to me, telling me about the incident and that he was now worried that she may have committed adultery on him. Now here she was sitting in my office telling me that she had and that because of it she thought she was losing her mind. What was going on inside of her head was driving her crazy. The Scriptures speak of the seriousness of sexual sins.

> "What? know ye not that he which is joined to a harlot is one body? for two, saith he, shall be one flesh."[159]

When a man and woman come together in sexual union there is a joining, that goes much deeper than just a physical bonding. It is a spiritual experience. It is a joining together of the two separate souls into one. The union of a man and a woman is a very serious binding, one that God has designed to last a life time. Part of the wonderful grace of God is that when a man and a woman join together the two become one.[160] There is a permanent union that is formed between the two. Breaking the bond is very severe causing great pain and a tearing of the soul and spirit of the two. When the

---

[159] 1 Corinthians 6:16
[160] Genesis 2:24

man and woman come together, God unites them together at all levels; mentally, physically, spiritually and in soul. When a man and woman make vows, committing themselves to one another and then consummate it, a bond that transcends mind and body happens. They are joined together spiritually and physically into one, new creature. This is how a man and a woman complete each other. They become joined and attached with an unseen yet unbreakable bond. That is literally what the definition of woman means, that which completes man.

The soul of a person in theology is referred to as, the volitional[161] aspect of the trichotomous[162] make up of man. It is the soul that works with the spirit making the two one. The soul is the part of a person that joins the flesh to the spirit. Just as the temple of God was made up in three parts; the holy of holies, the inner court, and the outer court, so also, the human being consists of three parts. Look at the following:

1) The Body is the outer court of the temple

2) The Soul is the inner court of the temple

3) The Spirit is the holy of holies of the temple

---

[161] Volitional means the decision making part of man. It is his soul
[162] Trichotomy means man is made up of three parts; body, soul & spirit

The holy of holies, is the place where the Holy Spirit of God dwelt inside the temple. When the Holy Spirit of God enters into a person it yokes itself to our spirit. God joins His Spirit to our spirit making our spirit the holy of holies inside the temple of our body. This is the part of man where God speaks to us through. He speaks to our spirit with His Holy Spirit and also guides us with the Holy Spirit through our spirit. This is the tie between God and us. This is where our fellowship with happens. By yoking himself to our spirit God fellowships with us, leads us, guides us, comforts us, and does the efficacious work of the Holy Spirit in us.

The second area of the Temple was the inner court. This is where the Word of God was read to the people. This was the area where teaching happened and also decisions were made. It was in the inner court of the temple, where the listeners would decide to, either *obey* God and his Word, or they would choose to do their own will. This is the part of the individual that is called the soul. The inner court is where we decide to either obey God or give into our flesh. It is in the inner court of our body, the temple of God that the war between the flesh and the spirit takes place. When a person gets a stronghold in their life it is because an unholy practice has come from the outer court, into the inner court. Christ will come into the inner court of your soul and will drive out the evil inhabitants so you can properly worship and serve the Lord God.

The last of the three parts of a person is the outer court. In the Jewish Temple the outer court was where the Gentiles and uncircumcised heathen were allowed to gather and to conduct all manner of business. During the time of Christ there was even a group of shops located in the outer court called the Bazarre of Annais. It was like today's shopping mall. Our outer court is our flesh. The flesh is at enmity against the spirit, this means the flesh is an active enemy against our spirit and the Holy Spirit of God. The flesh wars against the spirit and the spirit wars against the flesh.[163] Evil spirits will work through our flesh, to try and tempt us to sin in order to separate us from the power of God, in our life.[164] Spiritual warfare problems occur when we open the door to the inner court of our hearts by sin habits or ungodly practices. When the enemy comes in he will create a stronghold in our lives.[165] They not only come in but then they set up business! When an unholy bond or attachment becomes a stronghold it will begin to work towards the ultimate destruction of the individual.

In the case with the adulterous woman, we prayed together and she asked the Lord to forgive her for the sin of adultery and fantasizing and to take the sword of the Holy Spirit and to sever her from all unholy ties and attachments between her and the man she had committed adultery with. We then asked the Lord to cast out all of the spirits associated with the sin of adultery and to send them where the Lord would command them to go by the voice of his Holy Spirit. Next she prayed and asked the Lord to cleanse her in the blood of the Lord Jesus Christ and to seal her with the Holy Spirit, filling her in all of her empty places with the fruit of the Holy Spirit. We were not finished yet.

---

[163] Galatians 5:17
[164] Isaiah 59:1-2
[165] Ephesians 4:27

Next, I then prayed and asked the Lord if she had any introjects in her. Introjects are a demonic spirits that enter into a person, through an unholy tie or attachment. They will often carry the essence and character signature of the person with which the unholy tie or attachment has been made. She had several introjects so I asked the Lord to let her see them, which he did. When a person sees and introject it will often look like the person or sin that they person is under the influence of. For instance, I asked a man who was addicted to alcohol if there were any introjects in him and he said that the Lord showed him a twelve pack of beer. He prayed confessing the sin of alcohol and asked the Lord to cast it out of him, cleansing him from all unholy ties and attachment and then to fill him in all of his empty spaces with the fruit of the Holy Spirit.

After the Lord showed the woman the introjects, I prayed and asked the Lord to bind the introjects, triple chaining them, and gagging them so they could not speak, and to place them in a hermetically sealed box. Next I asked the Lord to seal that box and to fill it with the blood of the Lord Jesus Christ and to cast it out of her never to return. Once again an introject[166] is an entity that enters a person when an unholy union happens. It can be from consensual sex, forced rape, being molested or any form of idolatry. This allows a demon to take a part of the essence of the individual and to enter into the other person. The demon will often take the appearance of the other person and then seek to effect the emotions and mind of the person entered.

---

[166] This is not mis-spelled it is introject

They can enter from many different ways to include rituals via proxy, where DNA is involved, or even by the eating of cursed food.

I remember a teenager who was brought to me by a member of my church. This young man was not a believer in Jesus Christ but he came to me out of desperation, to get relief from a song that was playing in his head nonstop. The song had kept him up all night and was even playing loudly in his head while he was at school. The music would not stop playing and it was very loud. The particular song plaguing the young man, was a demonic and blasphemous song sung by a band that was openly satanic. What I found interesting was that the young man was not interested in becoming a believer in Jesus Christ. I witnessed to him about Christ and I felt led to help him so I asked him, if I could have permission to pray for him in proxy with authority. He gave me the permission so I confessed on his behalf listening to that particular band and then renounced them on his behalf. I then asked the Lord to sever the unholy ties and attachments to this song that was playing in his head and to cast out any and all spirits associated with it. The young man looked up and said the music is gone. He left feeling a great deal of relief having experienced the severing of an unholy tie. The following is a list of ties than can be unholy:

1. Sexual ties
2. Relational ties
3. Religious ties
4. Familiar ties

5. Generational ties

6. Psychological ties

7. Financial ties

8. Emotional ties

9. Legal ties

Let me make this statement; Not all ties are bad. God has designed for us to have healthy, happy bonds with one another and with his creation. What happens is that the enemy will seek to lead the person into a sin that violates the law of God, in order to bring affliction and misery to them. God blesses us when we have ties or attachments that bring him glory. The enemy uses ties to bind and enslave the individual. The tie between Jonathon and David was a God blessed relational tie. When a man and a woman come together committing themselves to one another, asking for the blessing of God to be placed upon them, it is a blessed union. This is a proper soul tie; a bond that makes the man and the woman forever one.

1) An unholy tie occurs when God's laws are violated.

2) Unholy sexual ties are formed whenever two individuals join themselves together in sexual intimacy, outside of the marriage union.

3) Unholy relational ties are formed when we yoke ourselves together with unbelievers. One good example of this is when a Christian and a non-believer go into business together. This creates an unholy tie as it violates Gods word about being unequally yoked with unbelievers.[167]

4) Unholy religious ties that are formed when we join with a group that does not hold to the literacy of the Scriptures or violates some aspect of how we should engage in formal and public worship.

I have counseled at least a dozen Christian men, who have lost all of their life savings by violating this simple principle of business. God wants us to worship him in unity with brethren of like minds that are indwelt by the Holy Spirit. Two joined together that are led by the same spirit both with the mind of Christ. That means the bonds that we create should only be with born again believers that are committed to living for God and are seeking to honor Him with their lives. If we need a business partner, than we should only yoke ourselves to someone that is a committed Christian. This union is blessed by the Father.

We can even have unholy ties in the way that we seek to worship the Lord God. For instance, if we join ourselves to a religious group that does not preach and teach the whole truth of God's word, then we bring the curse of a unholy religious tie upon ourselves. I led three young people to the Lord just recently and I took the time to introduce them to the pastor of a solid

---

[167] 2 Corinthians 6:14

bible believing, bible preaching church but during the next week their friend convinced them to come to his church because the music and worship at his church were a whole lot of *fun*. When I ran into these three new believers the first thing I noticed was that all three of them had backslidden, their joy was gone and they were unsuccessfully trying to go back to their old ways of life. Because they hadn't been properly discipled; they did not know how to live in the truth of God's word. A person that is truly born again cannot fellowship in a house of worship, where the truth of God's word is not being preached and obeyed. They will starve spiritually and begin to die inside. Music and dancing are not ways to honor and worship the living God; they are the practices of the heathen. God's children are to come together in order to learn of Him and when they do sing; the songs should be songs of praise unto Him. They are to join hearts and hands in prayer for one another. They are to come out from amongst the heathen in order to worship and serve the Lord God.[168] They are to corporately work together to reach the lost. I find it strange that many people will not take the time to lead a person to Christ but when they find out that a person has accepted Christ, the first thing they try to do is to get them to come to their worldly church. That is the work of the devil and it creates an unholy religious tie.

I remember working with a young man who was having uncontrollable sexual urges. He was a virgin and had been saving himself for his fiancé. His intentions were, that he and she would both experience the intimacy of sexual union for the first time together after they were married.

---

[168] 2 Corinthians 6:17; Deuteronomy 11: Psalm 95:6

Hhe came to me because he had begun having uncontrollable lust for nearly every woman he saw. We prayed and asked the Lord why he was having this problem and he said the Lord showed him in his mind a Buddhist temple. I asked the Lord what this had to do with him. He then looked up and told me, that while he had been on a mission trip with the youth of his church they had gone to see a Buddhist temple. He and a few of the other teens had gone into a Buddhist temple and joined in the service thinking it was a *'cool'* thing to do. He even had pictures made of himself with his arm around one of the priests of the temple and pictures of himself bowing in prayer before a golden bell dedicated to their gods. He thought this was real cool and he even made jokes about it. The problem was that a spirit of adultery was passed into him from either, the monastery, the bell or one of the priests. The spirit of adultery had authority to enter into this young man because he unknowingly had committed spiritual adultery by entering into a place of false worship and then joining into fellowship with the priests there. Bowing before the golden bell in prayer had given legal authority to the demons to enter into him. By bowing he was showing submission to the spirits that they worshipped. What seemed like harmless fun opened a legal doorway for the demons to enter him. His bowing in prayer before their gods was an act of submission to their gods and open idolatrous worship. By this act the spirit which entered him had the authority to continually tempt him with lust because he had committed spiritual adultery. He had joined himself through this act with the unholy demonic spirit. This demon also did something else; it held the door open for other entities to come into him. They began seeking to tempt him in other ways. They led him down a path where the lusting for woman was a continual state of spiritual adultery and idolatry. Idolatry because he was worshipping the form of the goddess in his inability to keep from lusting for woman; actually any woman he saw.

The young man was not married but he had already vowed to marry a young woman. He was committed to her and they had already set the date for their marriage. God's word tells us that if a man looks on a woman and lusts after her, he has already committed adultery in his heart.[169] It only took a short while before the lust the young man felt when he was looking at woman turned into uncontrollable urges to go on the computer and look up pornography. When the confessions began to come out of him, he revealed that he would at times he would spend sometimes all night on the computer looking at pornographic filth. All of this sin had blinded him to how bad his condition had become. Rather than seeking help to get out of the bondage he sank even deeper into sin. The entities attacked his finances next be leading him into wanting to speak with woman in order to please himself while looking at pornography. This led him to begin calling adult services. These services charged him by the hour. He said that it became compulsive with him spending thirty plus hours a week with these female adult services. As the sins kept growing it was propelling him into a complete downward spiral where every facet of his life was being affected. Paying for this service caused him to fall behind on his bills. This young man, who had once had sought to live a life of purity now fell into a habit of compulsive

---

[169] Matthew 5:28

masturbation; four to seven times a day. It began causing him physical damage. His physical pain coupled with the humiliation of not being able to stop the sinful practices led the young man to start drinking. By the time he came into my office he had an alcohol habit to where he was drinking a minimum of a twelve pack of beer every night. The last stage of his sinful addiction was when he found himself going into adult bookstores to purchase pornographic videos and magazines. To this day when I think of this young man, I am amazed at how blind he was to his own sin. His life was in utter chaos and destruction. He was so blind to his sin that he had become very critical and judgmental towards other people. He began pointing out other peoples sins without ever seeing his own. It was at this point in the counseling session that he told me how furious he was when he found out that one of the deacons in his church was in the same adult store where he shopped for pornography! He said the deacon was in there buying adult books and videos. He wanted to turn the deacon into the pastor but since he was the assistant to the youth pastor he was afraid the deacon would turn him in and he might lose his job. This went on for several months. They would see each other in the adult store but they kept it a secret from others that they knew and especially from their church. Can you see the progression of sin and destruction that this one simple act of idolatry on a mission trip had caused the young man? From a DUI to frequent trips to the adult book store the demons that entered into him at the Buddhist temple set out to destroy his entire life and they were very effective.

Upon initial counseling the man withheld all information previously stated about the downward spiral and told me that the only problem that eh was having was with looking on women and not being able to not lust over them. He told me that he believed his lust problems stemmed from his church. He said that he believed his church was a spiritually dead church because it did not minister to him anymore.

Friends, this is another way the enemy will seek to destroy our lives; he will try to separate us from the church and the preaching of the gospel. In this young man's life it was deceptional misdirection. Deceptional misdirection is when the enemy blinds a person to their own sin and makes it look like the problem is with someone else instead. The person that has fallen into this type of in-depth sin will deny the problem or else they will accuse others. This young man chose the latter saying that he believed that the leadership of his church was corrupt because he had seen one of the deacons of his church in an adult video store buying pornography and that this must be the reason he was having such problems in his life. What he failed to see that he was also a part of the leadership in the church and was deeply involved in the very same sin! It was at this point that I confronted him, I asked him; *"Why were you in the adult bookstore?"* When I said that, it was like the lights got turned on. It took him a moment before he realized that he had spoken, without thinking it through; by his accusing the deacon he had condemned himself. I had personally prayed that if there was a demonic stronghold in this young man that the entity would over step it bounds and reveal itself. That is exactly what this spirit did. By accusing the deacon of the church of being in sin, he was revealing that he too was involved in the same sin. This is when I asked for his permission to pray with authority in proxy for him. He gave me the permission so I prayed and asked the Lord to bind the principalities, powers, rulers of darkness and spiritual wickedness in high places. The man told me that he could not hear anything and that he thought that he was going to pass out so I commanded the spirits to turn him loose and then bound the spirit from interfering in the man's ability to hear the truth. I then asked the Lord to come and create a place in his mind where the Lord Jesus could personally speak with him; which He did. Then I asked the Lord to reveal why the young man was having these problems in his life, it was then that the Lord brought to his mind the time that he went to visit the Buddhist temple. God revealed unto him that what he had done was spiritual idolatry and adultery. I then asked the Lord if there were any strongholds in him and he said the Lord affirmed that there were so I asked the Lord to him to be able to see them. I then asked the Lord to triple chain and to bind these entities, gagging them so they could not speak and then to make them bow before His holy presence. There were quite a few demonic strongholds. I then asked the Lord what he needed to renounce and confess in order sever the unholy ties and to get rid of these spirits. The Lord told him what he needed to pray so I led him in prayers to first confess all the sins he had been doing all the way from the beginning when de decided to go to the idolatrous Buddhist temple. Then he renounced the spirits and the sins and asked the Lord to take the sword of the Holy Spirit and to sever all the unholy ties and attachments and to cast the demonic spirits out of him that were associated with the sins. We then prayed together asking the Lord to cleanse him in His holy blood and to seal him with the Holy Spirit, filling all of his empty spaces with the fruit of the Holy Spirit. He then thanked the Lord for what He had done.

The young man was set free. He went to his pastor and church staff and told them his story, which was not received well. The deacon got very angry and called him a liar and the staff asked the young man to quietly leave the church and apologize to the deacon for accusing him, before he left. Sadly, they never questioned the deacon on his sin habits; instead they got rid of the young youth pastor.

I have worked with individuals who have come out of religions that are anti-Christian. Even though they were now born again, they felt strangely drawn back to their former churches. They knew that the practices of the church went against the Scriptures. For some reason, they could not break free from the feelings for the old religion. These feelings were trying to draw them back into the habits of their former religious life. Now that they had come to salvation and had left the former practices of worship, all the nuances of the former religion seemed incredibly attractive to them. This is similar to what the Hebrews experienced after leaving Egypt.[170] I've seen some people that could not get over the smells of the incense that would be burned, others were haunted by the contemporary worship, with its music and songs, still others missed the legalistically repressive forms of life. Old ways of life can be very hard to break away from. The worst of these habits

---

[170] Numbers 11:5

that I've encountered is the praying to idols or the praying to the spirits of departed saints or ancestors.

These are examples of religious ties that are unholy. They need to be dealt with by confessing them as being unholy and against the worship of the true God. The person needs to renounce in every way their form of false worship and all of its practices along with all of its unholy ties and attachments. Often the ties to these religions are very powerful, going back several hundred generations in the persons families line. Powerful bonds are formed between the demons and the individual when they pray to and request intercession from these idolatrous false gods. Praying to saints is idolatrous as it deifies them, giving them status as a false god. These wrong practices and bonds have to be severed and renounced. Also the individual may have familiars, from the false religion, that will need to be renounced and cast out.[171] A familiar is a demon that is assigned to a family line through unholy ties or practices. Familiar ties to demonic spirits are formed in one of three ways; by summoning them through idolatry or worship, by assignment through a ritual of dedication or a curse, or by vows that have been made by the person or a family member.

While studying the martial arts, I knew a man that formed an alliance with several animal spirits by summoning them. After the man was delivered from the animal spirit, the spirit of the tiger came back on several different occasions asking to be let him back in. The man could see him as plainly as

---

[171] Leviticus 19:31, 20:6: familiar spirits are spirits that are attached to a families blood line

you can see any other person, when he manifested he was just as visible and tangible as any other creature. The last time I spoke with the man he said that the spirit would still approach him from time to time in an attempt to get back into him. He also said that sometimes he found it hard to turn the spirit away. They were united for so many years, the spirit and the man had become close friends. The demon was his constant companions. For clarity; the demonic spirit was his friend and companion prior to his salvation. The tiger gave him incredible abilities in the martial arts, but this was demonic!

Jesus Christ is to be our best friend;[172] not an entity. The only spirit we should strive to have is the Holy Spirit of the living God. A student of this man also had the same experiences with animal spirits in which he gained the ability to levitate along with some psionic[173] mind abilities. Many people strive to acquire animal spirits because they give extra-ordinary abilities.[174] It is common through Wicca, Satanism, martial arts, or other false religions to have familiar spirits. Some of the abilities that they give are listed below:

1. The third eye: it provide insight and perception beyond ordinary sight like the ability to see aura's
2. Super strength; strength of 2 to 10 men
3. Levitation

---

[172] Proverbs 18:24
[173] Psionics is the ability to use the mind to do incredible things from astral projection to mind reading to telepathy, etc.
[174] For further study on this read my book, "The Beast Within," it describes anthropomorphism, shape shifters, changelings and vampires

4. Mind reading; able to read other peoples thoughts or memories

5. Telepathy; communicating to others with your mind

6. Telekinesis; moving things with your mind

7. Forth-telling; having visions and predictions

8. Sooth saying; also known as fortune telling

9. Aura reading

10. Some physical healing

11. Astral projection; projecting your spirit out of your body.

12. Shape shifting

13. Clairvoyance –the ability to gain information about a person, place, location, physical event or object through other than ordinary means. It is a supernatural ability to gain knowledge or to see something supernaturally.

14. Clairaudience –an extra sensory form of hearing.

The above list is in no way complete. There are other abilities that can be gained through unholy ties to demonic spirits. Though the abilities are incredible; they are demonic in nature. The spirit and the gift both need to be renounced by praying and asking God to sever all unholy ties and attachments with the sword of the Holy Spirit, and then commanding the spirit/s to leave you and to go where the voice of the Holy Spirit commands them to go. Then ask the Lord to cleanse the person in the blood of Jesus Christ and to seal them with the Holy Spirit, filling all their empty spaces with the fruit of the spirit. The familiar may return seeking entrance back into the individual. If this happens all the individual needs to do is to command the spirit to leave and go where the voice of the Holy Spirit sends it.

When a person severs familiar ties they will also need to pray and asked them to be severed on behalf of their children, family line and entire household. This even includes all their pets. Entities will often enter into the families pets until they can find a doorway to get back into one of the family members. It is important for us to live in the liberty that Christ has given us. In order for us to do this we must renounce all unholy ties and attachments to everything that is not of God. Being yoked to anything of the world will ultimately steal your joy and peace. The demonic realm will seek to manipulate our thoughts, emotions and lives, eventually bringing ruin to your life.

One last area that needs to be addressed is how the church can become infected through unholy ties or attachments of a single member. During my childhood my mother and I would watch scary movies together. We watched this show called "Creature Features." I remember watching one of those episodes where a vampire that came to a home but it could not enter into the home without being invited in. The vampire would not reveal this rule to the unsuspecting victims instead he would kindly ask the owner of the home, "Well aren't you going to invite me in?" The unsuspecting man thought nothing of it and said, "Oh sorry certainly, come on in." The vampire would then enter in and of course killed all of the occupants. Though this was a fictional movie it does hold a bit of truth. The vampire was a demon of sorts.

Demons are all around us but they do not have authority to oppress us, unless we give it to them through sin. They have several doorways in which they will try to enter into a person through. Some make an open commitment or vows to a demon through occult worship or practice. Others have simply believed a lie from the devil. By believing a demonic lie the person is rejecting the truth that God has for us. This happens often in churches. This is why a person should search the Scriptures to make sure that what they are hearing lines up with God's word.[175]

What those in the occult understand is this: When we ask someone to come into the church, unless we pray specifically against any spirits they may have attached to them, the entity that they possess will also enter into the church with them. This spirit will then be an access point that other demons use to come into the church through, in order to afflict the other members of the congregation. Also, if the person is involved in the occult, by inviting them in, you unknowingly have given them authority to do incredible damage to the church families, especially if you have given them the right hand of fellowship. You may be asking yourself; "Why would someone in the occult want to join our church?" They do not have a choice, all Satanist and devil worshippers are commanded to enter into Bible believing, preaching church's in order to undermine their work and to destroy them. They do not want to shut the doors of the church. What they want to do is to make the church, cold, dead and lifeless so that the power of God is not flowing through the members. This is the reason that satanic

---

[175] Acts 17:11

plants are sent into the churches. This is called the art of subterfuge[176] and will be addressed later.[177] When someone becomes a church member if they have not renounced the former things of old, they will bring the spirits attached to them into the congregation. Read the following Scripture:

> "But have renounced the hidden things of dishonesty, not walking in craftiness, nor handling the word of God deceitfully; but by manifestation of the truth commending ourselves to every man's conscience in the sight of God."[178]

The early church made a practice, that before baptism; the prospect would confess their former life, renouncing the things of dishonesty which often included idolatry and false worship. They would also burn all things that were cultic in order to rid themselves of every tie to their former life. I once led a young lady to Christ who was in her early twenties. She confessed that she came from a long line of satanic witches. She came to our home late one night and told me that she had destroyed their family alter to Satan in the basement of their home but she could not destroy the book from the center of the alter. It would not burn. I had a burn pile in the back yard so we went into the back yard and she threw it on the fire but the book literally would

---

[176] I had a deacon in my church that seemed to be the most dedicated and godly man in the church but he came to me and confessed that he was a generational Satanist and had been sent into my church to destroy it but God had convicted his heart. He taught me about how they continually practice the art of subterfuge.

[177] This is called subterfuge-the cult will send a person in so they can use legal authority to curse the church members

[178] 2 Corinthians 4:2

not burn. I poured lighter fluid on it all to no avail so I lifted my hands and renounced on behalf of her and her family and the book exploded in flames. Literally, flames went up no less than seven or eight feet in the air. As we went back into the home my phone was ringing so I answered it. Her mother, who just happened to be the head deacon in another local church and over the Sunday schools in her church, was on the other end of the phone. As she spoke her voice sounded like she was hissing. The woman was incredibly upset. I don't know how she knew it but she said, "you are going to pay for what you did; you will replace that book!" That book was a great source of evil for that family. I pray the rest of the family comes to salvation. The daughter who did was kicked out, which was not a bad thing as she applied and enrolled and was accepted into a good Christian college. Notice how cultic volumes were dealt with in the Bible.

> "Many of them also which used curious arts brought their books together, and burned them before all men: and they counted the price of them, and found it fifty thousand pieces of silver."[179]

Dr. Kenneth Copley speaks about four ways that churches become infected. These four areas all deal within the realm of unholy ties and attachments.

> "One way **the enemy infects a church is with counterfeit truth** — Satan can counterfeit the truth . . . . Consider the elder board chairman at Charlie's church who became involved with a young

---
[179] Acts 19:19

married woman in the church. That elder rejected God's truth about adultery's sin and consequences and accepted Satan's supposed truths. Though we do not know which counterfeit truths the church elder accepted, Satan offers several counterfeits: *"It's only a harmless, temporary fling; it could energize your marriage." "Look out for yourself. You have needs, after all, and surely God understands those needs have to be met." "God will forgive your indiscretions later. You can confess and agree with Him. There are many other counterfeit truths Satan feeds adulterers."*[180]

Secondly **the church becomes infected when members seek for counterfeit spiritual fruit**. "Satan can give great feelings, and believers, remembering feelings of joy, even ecstasy, upon their conversion, and first weeks with the Lord, may associate good feelings with spirituality. Some Christians crave those joyful feelings they experienced at the end of a weekend retreat the '*so called*' mountaintop high as proof all is right between God and them. With great feelings, those believers think they must be 'spiritual' because they '*feel*' so good. But feelings are fleeting and dangerous. Extreme emotional highs often produce extreme emotional lows. As believer's in the Lord Jesus Christ our lives are to be characterized as stable. Not from one emotional high to the next. These are deception experiences and our faith is not based upon a feeling. Feelings are of the flesh and we are to be walking

---

[180] Unmasking The Lies of Satan The Great Deceiver, — pg. 170 ; Kenneth Copley , Moody Press , Chicago , Illinois; 2001

according to the Spirit. We are to walk according to the truths and principles of God's word. Job was a man who had more than his share of troubles but there can be no doubt that he was a child of the living God. His life, as ours should be, was marked with sobriety. He did not base his relationship with God upon any feelings, good or bad, but rather upon the completed work of the Savior.

"Now faith is the substance of things hoped for, the evidence of things not seen."[181]

Look at this example of faith below:

"For I know that my redeemer liveth, and that he shall stand at the latter day upon the earth: And though after my skin worms destroy this body, yet in my flesh shall I see God: Whom I shall see for myself, and mine eyes shall behold, and not another; though my reins be consumed within me."[182]

Our salvation is one of assurance and trust, not emotions. ***Every false religion in the world is characterized by having moments of ecstasy and moments of despair***. This is not a Christian relationship with the Father. No, this is a bi-polar, demonic stronghold. The Bible tells us also of those who

---
[181] Hebrews 11:1
[182] Job 19:25-27

seek after a sign or sign gift as being given over to evil and demonic adultery.

> "But he answered and said unto them, An evil and adulterous generation seeketh after a sign; and there shall no sign be given to it, but the sign of the prophet Jonas:"[183]

This is the third point of infection which fills and overpowers many churches. When believers seek after power, which includes sign gifts, it corrupts them and shows that they are not being led by the Holy Spirit; rather they are being deceived by unholy spirits. The children of this world are lead about by the spirits of this world but the child of God has been illuminated by the Holy Spirit and been given the gift of faith. It is not a result of their personal works and it not based upon an experience they may or may not have had. It is based upon the finished work of Jesus Christ which is the Fathers gift unto us.

Dr. Copley tells of a ***fourth area of infection being an innate desire; a "hungering for something else."*** In other words instead of hungering for righteousness we displace a proper relationship with Christ and seek our wisdom from peers and others. When we take our eyes off the Lord and begin to look to others for guidance or to be a covering over us than everything that do in our Christian walk will be based upon the flesh rather

---
[183] Matthew 12:39

than the Lord Jesus Christ. As believer's our life is to be characterized by a dependence upon God. We are to live by faith in Christ Jesus we are to be walking by faith and trusting in the power of God and in His providential care. Looking to charismatic leaders will lead to wrong judgmental attitudes and a false sense of piety. This will also lead to a false joy that will end in depression. If we look to anything other than Christ and allow it to influence us in decisions or matters of life, then we have formed an unholy tie that will bring with it unholy attachments. That is why the justified walk by faith not by sight.[184] We trust Christ no matter what the circumstances or what the outcome of those circumstances will be. We continue to be faithful to God and hold to His word and teachings even when it appears that we stand alone. Elijah fell into this straight of despair.[185] He did not realize that God was doing a wonderful work and that he was the chosen vessel of God being used in that work.

Let me give you an example I learned on the farm. If you tie a hog to a sheep the hog will drag the sheep all over the pasture and when the sheep is too weak to fight back, the hog will turn on him and eat him. We are not to love the world for the world is our enemy.[186] We are not to trust in the flesh for the flesh wars against the Holy Spirit.[187] We are to resist the devil when he comes tempting us and he will flee.[188] Unholy ties and attachments will wear away at the believer's commitment to righteousness, until it is able

---

[184] Habakkuk 2:4; Romans 1:17; Galatians 3:11; Hebrews 10:38
[185] 1 Kings 19:4
[186] 1John 2:15
[187] Zechariah 4:6
[188] James 4:7

to lead them astray. Unholy ties and attachments are open doorways for the enemy to attack us and to establish strongholds through in our lives. If we are to tie ourselves to something, let it be the word of God.[189]

Let us yoke ourselves to Christ and continually seek to learn of Him.[190]
Let us learn to be content with whatever position in life that the Lord places us in.[191]
Let us draw near unto God and He will draw near unto us.[192]
Let us pray without ceasing and give thanks in all things.[193]

We serve a great and High God, Who is also our Bridegroom, the Lord Jesus Christ, and we are His Bride.[194]

---

[189] Deuteronomy 6:4-9
[190] Matthew 11:29
[191] Luke 3:14; Philippians 4:11; 1 Timothy 6:8; Hebrews 13:5
[192] 1 Samuel 14:36; Psalm 73:28; Hebrews 10:22
[193] 1 Thessalonians 5:17; Ephesians 6:18; Philippians 4:6
[194] Mark 2:19; Revelations 18:23

Weddings, Vows, and Summoning

This chapter is going into the darker side of counseling. It is something that a counselor needs to be prepared for when working with someone out of the occult; those who have cult ties. If a counselor is going to help someone get spiritually set free, at the minimum, they should have a basic understanding of the vow's, ceremonies, weddings, and summonings that are involved in the cultic religions. Just as we in Christianity have a walking, living fellowship with the true God and His Holy Spirit, those in the cult have interaction and fellowship with the demonic spirits that were cast down with Satan. The most important thing a counselor needs to learn is that the demonic realm is one of legalism. Demons know how to get authority to do what they do. They cannot just impose themselves upon an individual or their family members. They have to have a legal right, i.e. authority in order to work in the life of an individual. This is why the enemy looks for any legal ground to enter into, afflict or control those who are made in God's image. When someone in the occult comes to us for help in getting free, the legal ground the enemy has needs to be taken back![195]

When a person becomes born again they often believe that their life is going to become easier. But this is simply not true. Actually, what usually happens is just the opposite. Instead of having a continual peace of mind, they began having nightmares or internal struggles and internal stress for

---
[195] Ephesians 4:27

which there is no explanation. Sometimes they may experience moments of uncontrollable bouts of anger for which they have no explanation, or suicidal urges, or depression. This is called spiritual warfare. This believer has come under attack and if they or their family have roots in the occult, then the battle can become very intense. The Devil does not like it when one of his children seeks to leave the family of darkness. Though we are all children of the devil before we come to salvation there is once difference between those that are raised in a cultic family, they have been dedicated to a demon and have made vows to the demon at some point in their life.[196] The enemy will still want to control and influence the person's thoughts. Conflict occurs because the person has the Holy Spirit of the living God in them, which is seeking to lead and direct them but the ties to the demon, is allowing the demon to also influence the person. This creates an inner power struggle. While the enemy will try to hinder the Christian walk, remember this truth; Greater is God's Spirit in his child than anything of this world.[197] It is important to understand that strongholds do not just leave, unless God commands them to. We have all seen how quickly the power of God changes a person's life, the moment when they are born again. But when a person has made vows and has partaken in rituals to demonic forces the demons will not come out until every legal technicality and all the authority that they have given has been renounced and removed; even then sometimes

---

[196] Leviticus 18:21; Deuteronomy 18:10; 2 Kings 16:3, 17:17, 21:6, 23:10; 2 Chronicles 33:6; Jeremiah 32:35; Ezekiel 16:21, 20:26, 31, 23:37
[197] 1 John 4:4

they will only come out by praying and fasting.[198] These forms of devotion are rituals that the individual has personally been a part but also include those that have been done on their behalf; some have been done for them by their family members prior to birth. For instance, when a child is sprinkled by a priest, he asks the parents if the baby believes and they state on behalf of the infant that the child does believe. This is a ritual via proxy. The parents are speaking on behalf of the child and are giving the priest authority to baptize the child. The Mormons baptize via proxy. They will have a individual stand in on behalf of another person, who is not even present and then they will baptize that person on behalf of the one not present. This is a ritual via proxy.

Many rituals of authority are often performed without the person's knowledge yet in the demonic realm if the one replacing them in the ritual has any ties, attachments or yoking of authority with the missing person it is valid. A tie can be made by something as simple as a person joining themselves to a false religious group. Many groups and organizations have oaths and vows that on the surface seem innocent but actually by making vows or going through induction ceremonies, even by doing the simple act of giving a penny or donation to their cause will create a tie and/or attachment to the group or organization.[199] Some groups will initiate the person in extreme ways, like having the person taking part in the murder, sacrificing, and often consumption of an animal or human. Dealing with

---

[198] Matthew 17:14-21
[199] When you give a donation it creates a financial tie to that group or organization

those coming out of the occult is not something for the squeamish, it is a calling. Counselors mentally cannot deal with some of the horrendous things that may surface from a person's past.

Early in my ministry during a counseling session with a person who was SRA-DID[200], the individual had brought another Christian with them as a prayer partner. I have always made it a practice not to meet with an individual alone so that it protects their testimony and also mine. I want everything to be open, honest, and safe and secure for myself and the client. They brought their own prayer partner from the church, which stayed in the room with us during the session.[201] Neither of us was prepared for what happened in the session. An alternate personality came to the surface that had been an active member in a satanic coven. I lead the alternate personality to the Lord and then instructed her to confess all the sin's that the Lord brought to her mind so that after healing and forgiveness she could be integrated back into the life essence of the individual. The sins she began renouncing were incredibly horrifying. As the person began a long and detailed prayer, her prayer partner became physically sick and horrified by what can only be described as, incredibly evil and inhumane. The lady who was her prayer partner was unable to finish the session. They both left but she came to me later that week saying she could never be a prayer partner to anyone again because of what that one session did to her mentally and physically. She told me that she could not get the thoughts, of what she

---

[200] Satanic Ritual Abuse-Dissociate Identity Disorder
[201] I will not counsel a person alone for my and their testimonies sake.

heard that day out of her head. I had to counsel her and lead her in prayers for the Lord to take the thoughts out of her head and to restore peace and sanity to her mind. Let me just prepare you; some people simply cannot handle what may be confessed by those coming out of the occult.

Weddings in the occult are very common. Even in the Masonic lodge and the eastern star the individuals are wed to demonic entities/un-holy spirits by the vows that they make and the rituals/ceremonies that they go through. One SRA-DID client that I worked with, had been prepared from birth for a specific position of use by the families' coven.[202] She had been wed to her first principality[203] at the age of six months. The coven had performed a ritual with the parents giving her in marriage to a prince demon. This happened while she was an infant. They placed her on the table as an offering to the demon and then placed in her bottle; not only milk but also animal DNA[204] and human blood.[205] This was so the child would drink all three of the components. The cult then performed the ritual while the infant drank the formula. She was then wed at three other times in her life to other prince demons. I believe it was a four faced cherub and each one of the demons were one of the sour aspects of the same cherub. I understand that this will sound bizarre to many of you but actually this is very common. I worked with another young lady from Sri Lanka that was bathed in milk

---

[202] SRA-DID means satanic ritual abuse dissociate identity disorder, These people are called survivors because they survived the circumstance with the use of their minds.
[203] Principalities are demonic ruling spirits
[204] From an animal sacrifice
[205] The human blood creates a link between the child and the person and also gives the blood donor authority over them, for instance in vampirism they will suck blood directly from the fingertip of the cult leader/head vampire.

from slain goats in order to dedicate her unto the goddess. This happened in a local church where the priest was also a cultist.

In covens, they will take a child at different ages, and from early infancy they will begin to split the mind through the use of trauma to dissociate the child. Many that do this to their children do not understand that this is what happens to the child's mind, they are simply performing sexual practices or painful acts in service to the demons they worship. They will call upon their gods, summoning the spirit of the demon to manifest and will then dedicate the child to the demon in an official wedding ceremony which is consummated through molestation, bestiality or incestuous practice. The trauma will split the child's mind creating two personalities. One side will hold all the pain and shame and will be used for incest and other areas of the demonic worship while the other personality will live and function in society. By splitting the child's mind, it gives the demon incredible authority over the person. What is worse is that the presenting personality that is not associated with the abuse will not know anything about the cultic side within them; it is a demonic stronghold. Until the dark part is brought to salvation, renouncing the rituals and praying for the ties to be severed, they will be under the influence of the demonic entity. They will also be a target for continual abuse.

I have known many counselors that could not understand why they could not get a person set free. The problem was that the stronghold was not attached to the person they were working with but was actually attached to a different personality that was hidden in the recesses of the person's mind, in the no-conscious part of the brain. A person has to renounce all of these vows if they want to be set free. Unholy ties and attachments take many forms, to include; vows made to church organizations that are un-biblical in belief and/or practice and also brotherhood organizations which deal with secrecy. When I talk about these unholy ties and attachment I am not saying the person has not been born again; what I am saying is that they will have areas of their life that remains in bondage until the vow is broken. When we wed yourself to the Lord Jesus Christ, because He is our husband, he can make any and all vows null and void. Read the following:

"When thou vowest a vow unto God, defer not to pay it; for he hath no pleasure in fools: pay that which thou hast vowed. Better is it that thou shouldest not vow, than that thou shouldest vow and not pay.

And if she had at all an husband, when she vowed, or uttered ought out of her lips, wherewith she bound her soul;
Nu 30:7 And her husband heard it, and held his peace at her in the day that he heard it: then her vows shall stand, and her bonds wherewith she bound her soul shall stand.
Nu 30:8 But if her husband disallowed her on the day that he heard it; then he shall make her vow which she vowed, and that which she

uttered with her lips, wherewith she bound her soul, of none effect: and the LORD shall forgive her."[206]

The Lord God takes vowing and the making of oaths to anything very seriously but my friend; any vow made before you came to salvation is made null and void by Jesus Christ when you confess it and renounce it.[207] The demonic realm knows that vows and oaths give authority and control. Every vow that a person makes to the Masons, Rainbow Girls, Sons of Demoley and Eastern Star will give a demonic entity power over the individual. The vow can be of any type or nature. For instance; it can be anything from a religious vow of poverty, (which is a form of self cursing), to vowing to never being hit by anything ever again. Each vow carries the weight of what is being said and then joins to the vow a set of consequences if the vow is not met to the letter of the law. By not keeping the vow completely according to the demonic spirit of the law it is a voluntary self imposing of legal authority over that part of a person's life. The fallen angelic realm knows this. Evil angels will use any legal issue to their advantage, in order to bring a curse against someone or to gain access to a person. Through the power of a vow, they can take control of the person's thoughts and decision making abilities. The amount of damage they can do to the individual and those around them is incredible. The way a person removes authority of the vows and their ability to control is by confessing and renouncing the vow

---

[206] Ecclesiastes 5:4-5; Numbers 30:6-8
[207] 1 John 1:9

with the authority it has over them, and lastly the person openly stating that it no longer has any place in their life. After doing this, the person needs to ask the Lord Jesus Christ to sever all unholy ties and attachments to the vow and whatever the vow was made to and then in turn, give Jesus Christ full authority over that area of their life. For instance, if they are renouncing being wed to a spirit they need to renounce, not only the spirit, but the ritual and the vows that were performed which joined them to the entity. The person may need to get very specific, in renouncing the parts of the ceremony that happened. The following is a list of the things that may need to be renounced.

1) The location where it happened
2) The ground upon which it happened
3) The people involved
4) The instruments that were used
5) The day upon which it happened
6) The entities that were involved
7) The name of the ritual
8) The vows made
9) The authority figures and the cult that were involved

After renouncing everything, the person will need to announce their position in Christ and His authority over them and this area of their life. They need to openly confess that Jesus Christ is their Groom and then they need to openly and willingly submit themselves unto him as His bride.

This brings us to the third topic for this chapter; summoning. This is the most misunderstood of the three; rituals, vows and summoning. Whenever a spirit is summoned, it will come. You do not have to see it or feel it but trust me it is there. This is why the Bible tells us not to even mention their name.[208] The demonic realm looks for opportunities to come and have ground in a person's life. Demons will even look for ways to obtain authority over territories, such as a plot of ground, a home, city or state. That is why some board games, role-playing games, and even children card sets, are so dangerous; they cause the person to say the name of an entity which will summon it! It does not matter, if the person thinks they are only playing a game such as dungeons and dragons nor does it matter if they do not believe in demons; when they say the name, the entity comes. If someone plays with a wee-gee board, tarot cards, an occultist game, or goes to a seer, practices or reads astrology or is an astrologer, psychic, or a palmist, they are going to have demons come to them, and often the spirit will enter into them.

I remember a referral I had received from a professional counseling clinic in the area. The person had told their psychiatrist that there was an evil presence in their home and that it was physically molesting them in their bedroom. The psychiatrist believed the person was suffering from delusions and believed the only way to prove that is was not really happening was to come to their home and show them that it was all in her mind. Much to the psychiatrist's amazement, when he went into the home, the spirit manifested

---

[208] Exodus 23:13, 34:14

and came at the psychiatrist. He literally saw it appear and then come at him. He rushed out of the home and said that this was out of his area of expertise so he referred the client to me. The lady called me and told me what was happening and stressed out she was afraid to go to bed in the house so I agreed to come right over. I went to the home and began by praying with the husband and wife and asked the Lord to reveal what was causing the demonic manifestation. What I discovered was that the demon began its assault's after the wife started seeing a palm reader. By going to a psychic/palm reader, the demons in the psychic had attached themselves to the lady and when she returned home they came into the home with her and then began sexually assaulting her. This happened because the diviner had summoned a *"dead"* spirit in order to get information for the woman.[209] Contrary to popular belief mediums are not channeling the spirit of a person that has passed away, what they are doing is voluntarily allowing a demon to possess them and speak lies and half truths through them. It was not the dead family member that appeared through the psychic; it was actually a demonic spirit that took the appearance of the dead family member and then it began lying to them. When she asked the psychic to summon her father, that had passed away, she partook in a practice that is condemned in the Scriptures and this opened the door for judgment to happen against her. The judgment came in the form of giving the demon that was summoned the authority to attach itself to the woman and then to enter into her home with her, where it took up residency.

---

[209] Deuteronomy 18:11; 1 Samuel 28:7

Séances will always open doorways that produce demonic spirits. If you dabble with psychics, diviners, palm readers or have séances, you will have demons attach to you! It's like my grandmother told me; son if you play with dogs you are going to get flea's.

When a demon enters a person through summoning, the person will begin to have unexpected complications and/or problems that will occur. Such things as mood swings, anxiety disorders, eating disorders, depression, an inability to focus, or understand God's word, an inability to pray, strong lusts or even uncontrollable urges can occur. The list of complications has no end. No matter how innocent something may appear to be, if it contradicts God's word, than it will open a doorway for a demonic stronghold to be established, in the person or their children. Let me give you an example of the dangers of wee-gee boards.

I had a woman call me about her daughter's unexplained change in behavior. I had known this family for over twenty years and the last time I had seen the girl when she was about five years of age; she was now fourteen. I arrived at the home and I can tell you there was a very powerful, evil presence in the home. We went to the girls' room and to me she looked possessed. She could barely talk with me. I found out that she and three of her friends had gotten a wee-gee board and that they went to use the board it began communicating with them without being touched. She said the last thing she remembered was the door and the window to the room slammed open just before an explosion happened that left all four of the teens unconscious. Her twenty year old brother heard the explosion and found them all laying out on the floor. The girl also had a strange burn in her leg in the form of a strange symbol. What had happened was a demonic entity appeared and possessed the girl. It took over her mind and body. She became very withdrawn, highly sexual and completely rebellious. She threatened her mother with a butcher knife and the son fought her off with a chair but still got cut in the process before they could get the door shut and locked. The girl refused to allow me to work with her and the family ended up having her committed to a mental facility.

Friends, cultic practices are very serious matters. They are not to be trifled with. Now let me give you a not so obvious example of a summoning. Take for example music. Music seems to be innocent but some music, not only summons spirits but by listening to a song dedicated unto a demon, can give the demon legal authority to enter into the listener. There are cultic bands that write music specifically for the purpose to dedicate it unto the demons they serve. Every time the song is played it is as a form of worship to the demon, with the listeners being participants. Let me say this again; while writing the music the band members will pray over the songs, devoting the music unto the god they serve. This gives the demon the royalties of authority to afflict and inhabit those who listen to it. This is a form of joining/yoking yourself with the band and the demon. The music world is being flooded with bands in the occult that are praying over their products and dedicating them to their demonic gods asking them to curse all who listen to their songs. It is actually incredible how much music is designed specifically for summoning spirits. I was called by a member of my church to come and see their teenage son. Now realize I knew this family well and the boy and I were quite good friends. I went to see the boy and he had dramatically changed. In a matter of a few months he had changed his bed room, with things that would typify it as being a normal teens room into a very dark and leery place. He had occultic symbols on the walls which were now painted black. Everything in his room was painted black! I asked if he would talk with me in another room and with the parents sitting in on the session we began. I first asked for permission to pray for him with authority in proxy, he gave me the permission. I began to pray and the boy became completely possessed. I commanded the spirit to be bound and turn the boy loose so I could talk with him. He was able to somewhat communicate with me at this time so I asked the Lord to reveal how the demons got the authority to enter into the boy. He told me that an adult that was in a position of authority over him had given him two cd's of a foreign band and that after playing them one time he could not stop playing them. His mother said that is right he would not turn them off. I asked to see the cd's and they were satanic worshipping black metal cd's. These cd's were designed with the purpose of summoning and infesting the listener with demonic spirits. It was not something I am speculating on, it was writing in English right on the cover of the cd. This band made sure that the listener knew that they worshipped the devil and it was dedicated unto the devil and that all who listen to were partaking in the worship of the devil. I lead the boy in a prayer of renouncing the band and music and asked the Lord to cast out the introjects, and the demons, sending them where the voice of the Lord commands. The boy was set free. I found out from him that this authority figure had given five different boys the same two cd's. each of those boys were changed. The parent did not even know this had happened.

Music is a very powerful tool that can be used for good or evil. In voodun[210] they play their musical instruments and dance for the purpose of summoning demonic entities. They begin the ritual and continue until a spirit appears and possesses one of the people. When the spirit appears they instantly stop playing their instruments until they know what type of demon has entered into the person. They stop playing because some demons are very malignant and dangerous and when the person become possessed if it is one of the dangerous spirits, they may attack or even try to kill someone around them. Those that are not possessed have to be ready to flee from the possessed person if they need to. If the spirit is not violent, the participants will resume playing the music associated with that particular spirit and then they will have a worship service with the god/demon present and in the midst of them, manifested in the body of the possessed person. This happens in many types of religion.

When a person listens to music that is openly carnal it will open the doorway for demonic influence. This is one of the greatest sources of demonic influence in the world today. Sinful music affects the minds and lives of all those who listen to it. Any type of music can be carnal. Some of the worst is that which is marketed as being Christian. I have heard many

---

[210] This is the proper spelling for this type of religion. It is a mixture of hoodoo and voodoo and Roman Catholism

songs from contemporary Christian artist that are not only carnal but some are completely blasphemous. Music, with what I like to call demonic beats, can actually manipulate and even control a person emotionally. Some of the most popular songs today openly talk about physically hurting others or using them for self-gratification. Just about any sinful practice under the sun can be found in music, glorifying sinful practices as if they are something to be sought after.

Not long ago a man and wife asked me to come speak to their son. What was once a gentle and good natured boy, had in less than three months time, turned into a very violent and rebellious young man. This boy said that he was a believer in Jesus Christ and had been attending church every service even when his parents would miss. When I prayed with him in front of the parents he became totally possessed by two high level demonic entities. I asked the Father to bind them, which He did and then I asked them to reveal their names and how they entered into the young man. Their names were the names of two very popular black metal bands. They said they had entered into him from listening to their music. A person, who was an authority and that just happened to also be in Wicca[211] had given him for free one of each of this bands cd's. The boy said that he could not stop listening to the cd's, he even played them at night while he was sleeping. (Sounds just like the story from before, doesn't it.) These two evil spirits were causing the youth to be extremely violent. He had already struck his mother and father on several occasions. I also learned during the session that

---

[211] Wicca stands for the group of individuals that all practice witchcraft

one of the two demons was a spirit of death and that they had both been working together to get him to commit suicide. They were putting thoughts in his head such as; "Your parents really do not love you; just kill yourself. No one cares about you anyway. You would be better off dead. Life is not worth living." This child confessed that he was on the verge of suicide. We prayed and he renounced the spirit of death and confessed to the Lord that it was a sin to listen to this Black Death metal music. He then asked forgiveness and renounced all of the spirits asking the Lord to take the sword of the Spirit and to sever all the unholy ties and attachments. He also prayed and asked the Lord to cast the spirits out of him and to seal him with the Holy Spirit, cleansing him in the blood of the Lamb of Calvary, and finally filling all his empty spaces inside of him with the fruit of the Holy Spirit.

So why did I give you two reference? To make a point; it is happening much more than what is commonly known. I can give you dozens more examples from personal experience involving both adults and child clients. There is a Christian practice of evangelism known as giving out Bible tracts. Bible tracts are pamphlets that are used as witnessing tools to tell the reader the gospel of Jesus Christ so they can make a personal decision about whether they would like to receive Him as the Savior. Faith in Christ comes by hear His holy word. Those in the occult also witness, except they use a more devious plan; they give out items that are cursed in order to demonize the recipient. Demonic spirits come when they are summoned. Music is one of the preferred methods of doing this with the youth today. When the song plays the music opens a doorway right into the person's mind allowing for demonic infestation and sometimes their total possession.

Let me re-emphasize this point: The Black Death metal music, these young men had been listening to, was specifically designed to summon evil spirits and these cd's were being given out for free by cultists. The bands did not hide the fact of what they were into; they openly boasted of their worship of Lucifer and that their music was devoted to him. As the child listened to the music it opened doorways into him. Then as the child began to repeat the cultic phrases, and sing the songs filled with hate, violence and filth, the demons were allowed to enter into him and to take control over him. The entities created a stronghold in the young man which resulted in his entire character changing into those depicted by the songs he was listening to. A metamorphosis occurred; he was becoming what he was listening to.

    Virtually any form of media can be used for summoning entities. There are specific cartoons, movies, and TV shows that have been written, with the names of demons as main characters in the script. When these shows are watched the names are being openly said which summons the demon into the room. It is a mass media way of bringing evil spirits into a person's home. Some cartoons have been prayed over and written for the direct purpose of opening doorways into the children that watch them so that evil spirits can afflict them. There are many famous movies, some dating back to the fifties and sixties with well known actors in them that show outright rituals of summoning. When these movies are played the ritual summons the fallen spirit into the person's home.

We have got to be careful with what we watch. The Bible tells us not to set any unclean thing before our eyes.[212] This is good advice to be heeded for the eye is often called the window to the soul; and it is.[213] What we watch, read or hear will directly influence our decision making ability. Just as music can affect us through what we hear, what we watch can influence our thoughts and can also allow demons to enter into us, through the eye gate. The person addicted to pornography will confess that it all began with a moment of temptation that turned to lust. Once the doorway is opened, the spirit will work on that one particular area of sin until it has became a habit that you are given over to. Then it is called a stronghold.[214] We must stand firm in the power of the Lord's might and resist the devil and he will flee.[215] This means that if you resist the temptation there will come a point where it breaks. The believer in Christ must deny the flesh, resist the devil and flee the world. These three are our enemies; we must recognize what we are being tempted or tried by and then deal with appropriately. I remember early in my Christian life of hearing a song that sang about how we need to guard our heart against the temptations that will tear us down. Make the decision today to take control of what enters into your ears and eyes. What is in our

---

[212] Psalm 101:3
[213] Matthew 6:23
[214] James 1:13-16
[215] Ephesians 6:13; James 4:7

heart will come out of our mouths when we speak.[216] Do the things that we take joy in, lift up our Savior or are they against Him, His word, and His Kingdom? We cannot have two masters in our life. We will either give into the temptations of the world, our own flesh or the devil; or we will rest in the goodness of our God. I pray you choose the Lord Jesus Christ. There is blessing and peace with Jesus. The god of this world seeks to destroy your life. Sin will make you pay a price that will cost you far more than a moments pleasure is worth.[217]

---

[216] Matthew 12:34; Luke 6:45

[217] Joshua 24:15

The Hidden Enemy

> For I know this, that after my departing shall grievous wolves enter in among you, not sparing the flock."[218]

The apostle Paul is warning the church about an enemy that was very real. Paul understood the enemy of the Lord. A sad reality that must be faced is that there are children of the devil that will come into the church of God with the driven desire to devour the flock. I have met many of them and have had the privilege of leading them to salvation. In my first two churches they were continually being sent into the church to destroy it but the power of God turned the attack of the enemy into a celebration; because they became children of God. Like the wolf that seeks to feed off of a flock of lambs these individuals will have no mercy. They have lives that are filled with pain and despair; that they are void of love. They do not have the capacity to give love because they have never experience it. It is this hatred for God, themselves and everyone else that internally drives them. Friends the only reason that we love God is because he first loved us.[219] We, who are the hands and feet of Christ need to show them the love of Christ with a sincere, genuine love for them. Our battle is not against flesh and blood but against the demonic forces of darkness that uses the broken and shattered

---
[218] Acts 20:29
[219] 1 John 4:19

life as a slave to do their bidding. Man was created and then given dominion over all creation. God gave Adam angels to do the work of regulating and controlling his creation. These angels rebelled against the true Lord God because they did not want to serve him, nor to give him all the glory he so rightly deserves. They hate God and they hate us. Rather than serving mankind they now seek to enslave him and destroy him. The Devil is damned and he wants to damn as much of mankind as he can. Do not be a part of helping others reject the Savior, be the hands and feet of Jesus, with the heart of Jesus. Show them the love of Christ.

The Lord tells us to love our enemies, to do good to those who despitefully use us.[220] This can be hard if you live by sight rather than walking in faith. These people will come into a church desiring to cause division. They will not be obvious in what they are doing. They will be very sincere. They will volunteer for ministry and will support the causes of the church; all the while they are cursing the members and the work. By causing disunity their belief is that it will disrupt the work of the entire cooperate body. The wolf will charge into a flock of sheep in order to separate the group to make it easier to kill them off, one by one. These workers of evil will separate the members in order to put their focus upon the weakest of the group. They will try to drain them physically, financially and spiritually. The individual plants, because they usually send in more than one, will each have their own method of attack.

---

[220] Matthew 5:44; Luke 6:27

Several years ago I had a woman that came to the church I was Pastoring. At the conclusion of the service she immediately came forward to accept Christ. The next service she informed me that she had made the decision to be baptized and that she wanted to have it done as soon as possible. Two week later she was baptized and a new member of the church. If you were to have seen this woman she dressed like a homeless person. She kept her head down, cried a lot and acted very needy and broken. She gave off the appearance of someone that had endured a very hard life; this was only her appearance. Actually she was very intelligent and sophisticated and a practicing witch of Satan.[221] She had a habit of continually call members or dropping in unexpectedly to visit them. She had a number of excuses as to why she would just drop in; many times she would bring them a gift or some food item. It was in the third month of her being a member of the church that disturbing things started happening. It started with different members calling to let me know that after she would visit them they would often be missing small items from their home. Many of these items were virtually worthless. Some where even garbage. For instance I had a man tell me that he saw her taking cigarette butts out of his ashtray and sliding them into her shirt pocket. I began to think that maybe she just had a habit of stealing; probably because she was raised quite poor. I remember one afternoon getting a call from one of the churches families claiming that this woman had come to their home, for an unexpected visit and that after she left they noticed that a

---

[221] I ran into her outside of church once and did not recognize her. The person with her introduced her to me and she acted like she did not know me at first. She was dressed like a super model and she looked like one. She was a very different person outside of what the church family knew.

very, very expensive item was missing from their home. They couple were furies, to say the least. I asked them if they called her to see if she had the item and they assured me that was the first thing they had done and she denied even knowing about the item.

Now understand, this couple were rather wealthy and they had a great deal of very expensive possessions. Everything they had from cars to jewelry was always first class and top notch and they made sure that you knew that when you were around them. Money was a very sensitive subject to them and I believe it was a stronghold in both of their lives. They insisted that I call her and confront her. I told them that they may have lost the item or misplaced the item so that unless they knew for sure that she had taken the item that it was not right to accuse her. They had no evidence except it was there before she came and it was gone when she left. I agreed to call her. Before hanging up the member told me that she knew that the visitor had stolen it and she wanted me to do something about it. Before I progress with the story, I would like to say that many times Pastors are burdened with problems that are not theirs to bear. It is wrong for members to try and drag a Pastor into something that is none of his business. If the couple had of had proof or evidence that the person was guilty than it would have been a different matter and I would have handled it biblically.

After the couple hung up I immediately called the accused member and explained what the couple had told me. The lady denied knowing anything about the missing property and then went into a whaling and crying fit about how terribly hurt she was that this person would even accuse her. I tried to console her but to no avail. In less than two hours time I began getting many, many calls from upset members sharing their concerns with me, on how deeply hurt and wounded this woman was by my call many of them insisting on an apology be given to her in front of the church. You can see how this got taken out of context and blown completely out of order. I had only asked her if she had seen the item and possibly taken it. I said it in a very kind and loving manner and let it go telling her that I took her word on the matter and that I was sorry for having to call her. Next I had called back the couple that lost the item and them that she denied any knowledge of the item and that I recommended they file a repost with the local authorities. They did file a report but they also left the church. Sadly not only did they leave the church but they decided it was best to take as many members with them, which was three other families. (Out of the four families only one is attending church of any kind now). The division had begun. This new member over the next few years would make it a habit of visiting ladies of the church. Later on she got married and her husband also began visiting members of the church. They became one of the most liked couples in the church. Still on occasion members would tell me that things would go missing, when she visited their home.

It was in the second year of her and now her husband being in the church that I had two separate ladies tell me that they believed she was taking hair out of their brushes. One of the ladies had even caught her in her bedroom with the brush in her hand taking the hair out and shoving it in her pocket. This lady asked me; "Pastor why would someone take hair out of my hair brush?" I was a state chaplain at this time and had worked with a great deal of people in the occult and it was then that I suspected this new member was a witch. I went with two of my deacons to visit their home. We knocked on the door and she answered and told us her husband was not home but he would be back shortly. I asked her if we could come in and talk with and she opened the door and let us in. One of the two deacons opened by stating that they wanted to discuss with her why she went into another members bedroom to take hair out of her brush. I had to use the restroom so I asked if I could use her bathroom and she told me where it was. As I was returning from the bathroom I opened the door to a bedroom and what I saw was very sobering. I called the two deacons and her to where I was so they could all see what was in there. Off to the side of the room was lingerie that had disappeared from my wife's drawer at our home. I do not know how they got it but here it was hanging over a painted pentagram on the floor. What was incredible is that the top and bottom were hanging there stretched as if a person was in them. To this day I still do not know how they did that. There was also another small table with a wax figuring that had hair and other things that had been burned in the center of it. There was a few other items in the room along with a cat that was incredibly vicious! It hissed and snarled at us and tried to drive us from the room. She became very serious and looked like she was demon possessed. She told me I should not have gone into that room! To make a long story short she confessed that she was a satanic priestess and that her mother was the coven's high priestess. She said her husband was a generational Satanist also. I confronted her with the truth of the love that Jesus had for her and also us of the church. She had been raised believing that she was a child of the devil and forever damned. I explained to her that before a person gets saved they are already condemned and are also a child of the devil but that Jesus can cleanse us from all of that and make us an adopted child of God the Father. She prayed to receive the Lord and burned all of her cultic items. Her husband did not come out of the occult and she divorced him later on.

Friends, this woman had been used as an instrument of unrighteousness by the devil. She was sent into our church to destroy it. Had I of handled this in the power of my flesh she may have never come to salvation. Christ died to save souls. A person's soul is of more value than the entire world. I ask you; was her salvation worth the problems and the loss of church members? I hope you can say yes she was worth the trouble.

I believe God allows these wolves to enter into our churches so that we can minister to them and hopefully lead them to Him for salvation. What greater thing than to see a pig or a dog transformed into a lamb? If we were honest we would admit that we were sin filled before God changed us. Our battle is not against other people, they are not our enemies. They are slaves bound to sin and followers of the god of this world. They need redemption and cleansing and that can only come through the Lord Jesus Christ. Friends we should not be surprised when the enemy comes into the midst. Wolves hunt and feed off of sheep. These wolves are of the father the devil and the works of their father they will do.[222] He was a liar from the beginning and they are also liars. Let us share with them the truth; Jesus is the Truth.

While growing up, I used to watch a cartoon of a wolf who was always trying to get around the sheep dog. This wolf would dress up in a sheep costume before sneaking into the midst of the flock. Once he got into the midst of the flock, he would snatch up one of the sheep and would then run as fast as he could to try and get away from the sheep dog. This was funny because the wolf was dead set on getting a meal of lamb chops but in the end he would only have turnips to eat. As children, these old cartoons were very enjoyable to watch. It was always comical and funny because the wolf always failed in his attempt to steal the lamb but no matter how bad it ended up he would always come back and try again. He knew the power of persistence. This analogy contains a bit of truth but in real life the wolf doesn't always fail. In real life, when a wolf enters a flock of sheep the sheep will scatter and then the wolf will take down one of the lone lambs. Sometimes a few wolves will kill an entire flock of sheep in one night.

Only God knows, how many families have been drive from churches? Members that have been hurt or wounded by fellow believers and as a result have turned their back on the worship of God. This should not be! How many churches have closed their doors, or how many believer's have had their lives destroyed by the enemies' infiltration. I spoke with a man that was the head deacon in his church. I later found out from his wife that they were both Satanists that had been sent into that church so they could

---

[222] John 8:44

undermine it and destroy it. He told me that it was the art of subterfuge. Subterfuge is when a person, couple, or group is sent into the church for the purpose of destroying it. I was told that in the satanic high priest's home, there was a room set aside for prayer. Every coven member and their spouse, had to come there weekly to spend one hour in that room, praying curses against the local churches, pastors and the gospel's effect in their area. It was their duty and obligation. He said that there were always a number of couples in that room, cursing the church 24 hours a day 365 days a year. He said every satanic coven had one of those prayer rooms. They take spiritual warfare very seriously! This man and his wife both came to salvation. I learned more about the mind and attack of the enemy from this former cultist than I ever thought possible. Friends we are in a battle for the souls of men and woman. It's time that we woke up and redeemed the time for the day is drawing near. Let us draw near unto God with pure hearts and let us be the light to a world that is so desperately in need.[223]

In the Lord's house the enemy will infiltrate with the pure desire of destroying the work of God. It is not by accident that this happens. These individuals are trained and prepared for the work of undermining the work of the Lord. They wish to stop the preaching of the gospel. They propagate false teachings and half truths. They curse and pray against the members of the church and take great joy in seeing ministries destroyed. These *"plants"* are sent into a church by their covens so they can destroy it from the inside. Like the worm that eats its way out of the apple, because it is hatched inside

---

[223] Ephesians 5:14-16; Colossians 4:5; Hebrews 10:22; Matthew 5:8; 9:35; 2 Corinthians 10:4; Isaiah 28:6

the apple and only has to eat it way out. They are planted in the church and then began eating it from the inside out.

While sitting with a group of pastor's several years ago we were privileged to hear the testimony of a man who had formerly been a Satanist. He told us that after he joined the satanic church, they helped him incredibly with his finances and even helped him start a very successful business. But he also pointed out that it was not free; he was expected to do his part in furthering the kingdom of darkness. They assigned him to a Bible believing, preaching, evangelistic church. He and his wife would daily curse and pray for the church to close its doors. They would pray for sickness to come upon the members and for the pastor and his wife to fall into sin, striking at the shepherd in order to scatter the sheep. He said that his assignment was to get as close to the pastor as possible, which he did. In two years time he became the head deacon, of this very large inner-city church. He then became the personal friend and confidant of the pastor, often giving him advice and counsel. He said he never missed a church service. The coven made sure that he and his wife paid the highest tithes in the church. They used this to win the leadership of the church over. Unfortunately man church leaders are won over by finances. He said that after he had built confidence with the individual members that he would look for opportunities to start *"little fires"* in the congregation. He looked for ways to deliberately create small areas of contention, without being noticed, in order to weaken the church, and to set spiritual traps for the members that were the pillars of the church. He wanted to make it so they would fall spiritually into sin. By targeting the strongest members of the church, he said he would be able to knock the support of the church out from under it so that the entire structure would collapse. The main intention was not in getting the church to close its doors, but more so, to lead the pastor and his wife into sin, so they could better affect the doctrine of the church along with its effectiveness in evangelism and outreach. He would say comments to people that he knew would gossip, so they would be the ones that started the contention in the church. He would say things like; "did you see sister ….'s skirt? Wasn't it rather provocative?" Or, "isn't brother ____'s daughter dressing risqué? She sure is a beautiful child." One of his best was; "didn't the pastor's message seem awfully dry? You don't think he may be falling out of fellowship with the Lord do you?" His wife was the nice person, she never gossiped or would repeat anything; and everyone knew it. She had a different plan of attacking the ministry of the church. She was a very attractive woman who would look for opportunities to brush up against the pastor. She would also drop in unexpectedly to visit him in his office to discuss personal issues, seeking to create a relational bond with him so that she could lead him into adultery with her. Realize that those in the occult have no problem with their spouse having adultery with someone else. It is even encouraged to further the kingdom of darkness. They also prayed against the Pastor's wife so that she would feel neglected and would become bitter against her husband being in the ministry and jealous of the individual members. Their desire was to separate her from fellowshipping with the members. This wanted to create a jealousy in her about sharing her husband with the ministry of the church.

Everything they did was with the direct purpose of taking away the unity and peace of mind of the church members and to replace it with bitterness, gossip and hypocrisy. This Satanist pointed out how he would deliberately talk about members and their children with his wife just loud enough for others to hear in order to get people to gossip. Remember Satan is the accuser of the brethren and if you can get God's people to gossip you have gotten them into a state of rebellion against the word of God. The sin of gossip is doing the work of Satan.[224] He said in the two years' time they had created enough contention and gossip amongst the members of the church they were assigned to that it went from over 400 members to only 78; and those that were left were becoming cold and dead. Remarkably though, after two years of doing this he came under conviction and gave his life to the Lord Jesus Christ. This is when he confessed to the church and the Pastor what he and his wife had been doing and how, if they were removed from the membership, the coven would send in other plants to take their place. He explained that they had a strategy in how they were to attack the church.

Whenever the couple was assigned to a church after becoming members the wife would immediately volunteer to work in the nursery, openly sharing her love for children. They did this knowing that most people are looking for ways to get out of doing the nursery work. By the second week after joining this church she had been placed, full time into the nursery. Her motive for entering the nursery was to pray over all of the children that were entrusted to her care. She did this to curse them in every

---

[224] Proverbs 6:16,19; Revelations 12:10

way possible. The husband began volunteering to do visitation and help set up the church. He even had his own set of keys given to him, which allowed him in any time he wanted. Some of the members knew that something was wrong with this couple but they never had the courage to confront them. It was probably because of the amount of tithes they contributed to the church. The idea of someone actually worshipping the devil seemed quite foreign to the pastor and the church's leadership. They had never dreamed that people would actually enter a church just to destroy it.

I spoke with another man who told me his job was to move into new areas, to plant satanic covens. Before his salvation he told me that he and his wife would go and pray in a special room every week for one hour to their fallen spirits. They would ask the demons to, bring sickness upon Christians in that area, and for pastors to fall into immorality so the Christian churches would fail, and have to close their doors. He said that every couple in their 200 member satanic congregation would spend one hour a week in that room praying against the churches of the Lord Jesus Christ. There were multiple prayers going up around the clock twenty four hours a day seven days a week.

When a Satanic plant enters the church, they have a well thought out methodology in how they attack. They will pray for people to not be able to focus on the sermon or to be able to clearly hear the pastor's message. They will pray for the babies to cause distractions. They want children to be so loud that they disrupt the message and irritate the other members in the service. Before church they would pray a curse into their hand, with a seal that would release the curse into the first person that they shake hands with. They would pray that the curse would grow with each hand shake. The type of curse is designed so that after the cultist shakes hands with someone, the curse will pass into that person and then it will reproduce and go into every person they shake hands with. It is a chain effect that links them all to the sin of the spirit from the curse. This is called transference. It is where a spirit can pass from one person into another by the act of extending them the right hand of fellowship, giving them a hug, or by the giving of a kiss. This is why you should beware of hugging others. Many spirits are transferred to unsuspecting believer's through handshakes and hugs. These plants will get a key to the building so they can enter into the church whenever they want to, in order to do rituals. They will carve or draw symbols in places that are not likely to be noticed. These marks are places used to give doorways for the spirit of the mark the authority to enter in through the mark. You can pray the spirit out of the building but if you do not cleanse the mark from the facility the spirit will just come back. I have personally found demonic symbols drawn and/or carved into the bottom of tables in the Sunday school rooms and on the back of bathroom doors, under the carpet in the sanctuary, etc. They place them out of site. They can put them anywhere. I have also found them on the pews and floors of the church. They will do whatever they can, to destroy the worship service. These satanic plants are not satisfied with just attacking the church service; they also infiltrate the homes of the strongest believers.

It was about 3:30 in the afternoon and for some reason a wave of weakness swept over me. I felt like all the energy in my body had been drained from me, so I told my wife that I felt sick and I went to lay down. As I lay down a cold sweet broke out over my face and that's when it came through the window. Something black slithered into my bedroom window and wrapped around me. It held me so tight that I could not breathe. Though no words were spoken; I knew I was going to die. This entity was killing me by crushing me, I was suffocating. I could not breathe let alone talk. I screamed out in my mind for the Lord to help me and instantly a bright light surged from my body casting it off of me. It slowly left out the same window it came in. While the entity was on me, I knew I was going to die. It was like death had wrapped around me. I later learned that this was leviathan, a spirit that is sent to physically assault or kill someone. This happens when a coven does a ritual of summoning and then sends the spirit to try and kill someone. This was my first real taste of the enemies attack upon my physical body. If I would have died it would have appeared as a heart attack.

Satanic plants will seek to gain entrance into your home. They cannot enter your home, with demonic authority, unless you invite them in. They have to have your authority to enter your home and bring the demonic spirits in with them. They will go into your bathrooms, to take hair from your hair brushes that they will use in rituals against you and your family. They will take prized possessions to use against you. It is not uncommon for them to give you an item that they have cursed so they can attack you from within your home. They will take needles they have cursed and will shove them deep into the couches or furniture so they cannot be found. To someone not in the occult this will sound incredibly strange, but you have to understand in the satanic kingdom; you either serve Satan with all your strength or you may be the next sacrifice!

Once a cultist has entered your home with authority they can astral project back in with their demons at night while you are sleeping in order to attack all of the people in the home. They will enter into the dreams of those in the home while they are asleep and will also affect the thoughts, moods and emotions of all in the house while they are awake. Common forms of attack are:

1) Reoccurring nightmares that seem real
2) Being pinned down in bed by an unseen force
3) Being Molested in bed
4) Not being able to breath
5) Feeling exhausted when you wake up from nightmares

During this period of my life I was planting a church in an area known for having a large number of people involved in witchcraft and Satanism. The spiritual warfare was incredible. I remember how for almost three months I would wake up at 12:35 am with my lungs filled with water. There would be so much water in my lungs that the water would shoot out of my nostrils, like two water hoses, covering my clothes and the bed spread. I would be choking for air pleading with the Lord in my mind to save. God would stop the attack and I would be able to breathe again. I could not lie back down or go to sleep again or the attacks would start happening again. I would have to sit up to 3 am and then I would feel the evil leave. I would then be able to go back sleep again. It happened every night. I would wake up and roll straight off the bed onto my knees so the water would shoot out of me until I could breathe again. I even saw a doctor who could find nothing wrong with me. It was supernatural! I would not drink anything for hours before going to bed, so that I would not have any extra water in me but still I would be flooded with water. It was like I was drowning. The best way I can describe it is that is seemed like a water hose had been pushed into my lungs and then turned on full blast. The amount of water coming out of my lungs through my nose and mouth would be at least a half a gallon or more. It was at this point that I called a former Satanist who now works in Christian ministry. He informed me that what was happening to me was that a coven were meeting and performing a ritual to drown me in my sleep. He said the way it worked is that they would gather in a circle looking at a picture of me and then they would chant. They would all chug water in between chants asking their demon to transport the water from their mouths and into my lungs, in order to drown me. He said that if one of the Satanists was a hidden member of the church that I was Pastoring and had been invited into our home by me, than it would give them the authority to assault me. The unknown member would have a link/yoke to me, allowing the demon to transfer the water into me. If I would have died it would have appeared that I had died from pneumonia. That night I prayed for the Lord to sever me from all unholy ties and attachment and to protect me from this ritual. I have not experienced that problem since.

When you allow a coven member to enter your home, it gives them authority to do incredible harm to your entire family. The following is a basic way of praying protection over your household. If you believe you are under demonic attack in your home than I suggest that, each night when you go to bed, as the head of the household, pray the following prayer. If the husband will not pray, than the wife should pray for him and the children. Pray this:

> Lord Jesus Christ I pray asking that you cleanse this home from anything evil. I pray that you reverse any curses, hexes, vexes, spells, chants, incantations, hybrids, or any other evil force sent against me, my family, or the church. I also ask that you reverse any prayers against me, my family, or the church and cancel any and all assignments against us. Lord Jesus will you please send away any and all evil assignments against us and place holy elect angels of rank and authority to stand watch over us as we sleep. Lord would you also cleanse all of our property with the blood of the Lord Jesus Christ from the four corners to every inch within it. Next Lord Jesus Christ will you cleanse my home from the top of the roof to the bottom of the foundation and everything else within the home. Will you cast out any and all spirits and place a force field around my home so that no one and nothing can enter in physically, astral, or ethereally. Keep out all astral projected entities weather human or other. Please completely seal our home. Lord

I also pray that you would release the fullness of the Holy Spirit of truth, power and a sound mind within our home this evening. Touch our minds so that as we sleep we have sweet dreams and peaceful rest until the morning hours. Equip us so that our minds are stayed upon you and prepare us that we will seek you early in the morning when we arise. I pray that as king Solomon was surrounded by mighty men with drawn swords that you would also surround the beds of each of us this night with holy angels of rank and choosing by your hand so watch over us until we rise, for your angels camp around those that fear you and you deliver them.[225] We thank you for hearing our prayers and trust in You, our Lord and our God, Amen.

I pray a prayer similar to this most nights. I recommend you develop your own prayer as you are lead by the Holy Spirit for cleansing and protection in your home every night.

As you've notice by now I have been redundant on several topics in t his book I believe that some things are worth repeating so let me give a bit of a recap. We need to understand that our battle is not against people, even if they are in the occult. Our real enemy is the satanic kingdom upon this earth lead by the various demons in ranking positions. We need to pray for the salvation of these individuals who are trapped in false religions. Many of them are hurting and looking for a way out. I remember how a man and wife who came out of the occult described it. They said you either served Satan

---

[225] Psalm 34:7

with your whole heart or you may be the next sacrifice. They were serious! The religion of Satan is one based on fear and pain. God does not give us the spirit of fear but his Holy Spirit does give us authority, the ability to love and a sound mind.[226] A man that I lead to the Lord told me that he had been sent to kill me by his satanic organization because I was causing them problems by witnessing to their people. After visiting the church three Wednesday evenings in a row, he came to salvation. He said he had never felt such love and did not know how to handle it. He was not a mere dabbler in the occult but had come from a family that had been committed to and involved in, the worship of Satan for many generations. When a satanic church is in an area they are expected so suppress the preaching of the gospel. They encourage churches that water down the gospel or that preach a social gospel. They are against churches that preach the literalness of the Scriptures. They are given over to the work of the prince of darkness.

Occultism is any practice seeking power or direction outside of the true God's will, to include, but not limited to, seeking direction from spirits. The question is often asked, "How do you minister to someone coming out of the occult?" The answer is quite simple; just as you would anyone else. You teach them the truths of God's word and pray asking the Lord to apply it to their hearts.

"And ye shall know the truth, and the truth shall make you free."[227]

---

[226] 2 Timothy 1:7
[227] John 8:32

"They must be born from above."[228]

How do you identity someone that is involved in the occult in the church? The true Satanist will not reveal themselves. They will seek to be as normal as possible while doing their dirty work. The one in Wicca or the Occultist can be identified by clothing they wear, jewelry or identifying marks. They will live very secretive lives and may often show un-Christian attitudes. Their lives will be strongly tied to the calendar. Sometimes by simply asking them they will admit it. It is not uncommon for a cultist to become so demonized that they cannot hide the darkness in them. I remember once praying for the Lord to strike down any plants that would seek to disrupt the church service. A very beautiful young woman who would sit right in front of the pulpit grabbed her stomach as soon as I started preaching. She then let out a growl and began to utter loud obscenities while I was preaching. Everyone sitting there heard her! She looked up at me filled with such hatred that if she could have attacked me she would have. She had to leave the building in order to stop the pain. She could not walk on her own but had to be carried out under each arm. She was screaming; "Get me out of this building!" As soon as they got her out the door, she stood straight up, completely relieved of the pain so what did she do? She turned around and came back in. She took no more than two steps inside the door and then feel to her knee's growling for them, (the two individuals who had helped her out the first time), to get her out of the building. Now when I say

---
[228] John 3:3

growling, I mean just that she sounded like an animal! As soon as she was out the door she was fine again. She never came to the church again. She did ask to meet with me so I took another counselor with me to meet her. What the church did not know was this lady was a high priestess who revealed to me in front of a witness, that she had been sent to the church to destroy it. She was very angry because she had been set to set me up sexually. Her husband had even tried to show me provocative pictures of her but I refused to look and rebuked him. She was an unbelievably beautiful woman but I was committed to the Lord and my wife. When she said that she was supposed to set me up for an affair she snarled out; "you are too much a man of God!" I told her I had given my life to the Lord and I was faithful to him and that was why I was faithful to my wife. That night she astral projected into my bedroom and woke me up threatening that she would destroy me and the church. I prayed and asked the Lord to take her out of my home, which He did. I then got up to think about what had just happened and as I went into the kitchen my guest, the other counselor, was sitting up at the dining room table and he said, " . . . . was just here." I said, I know but the Lord made her leave. She had woke him up also, to threaten him prior to coming into my room.

To give you an idea of what a Satanist believes I have listed below the nine satanic statements.

THE NINE SATANIC STATEMENTS

- Satan represents indulgence, instead of abstinence!

- Satan represents vital existence, instead of spiritual pipe dreams!
- Satan represents kindness to those who deserve it, instead of love wasted on ingrates
- Satan represents undefiled wisdom, instead of hypocritical self-deceit!
- Satan represents vengeance, instead of turning the other cheek!
- Satan represents responsibility to the responsible, instead of concern for psychic vampires
- Satan represents man as just another animal, sometimes better, more often worse than those that walk on all fours, who, because of his divine spiritual and intellectual development, have become the most vicious animal of all!
- Satan represents all of the so-called sins, as they all lead to physical, mental, or moral gratification!
- Satan is the best friend the church has ever had, as he has kept it in business all these years!

Those involved in Cults tend to have their lives structured around events, cycles of stars and planets, and calendars. Birthdays are always a big celebration to the family members.

When you are dealing with someone coming out of Satanism, whether it be the worship of Lucifer, Moloch, Baal, Baphomet - the god of the masons, Zeus or any other god, there are certain things that you can expect. The cults are religions based on power. They seek to empower those that practice them, over others, or their environment. For this reason they draw weak minded people into their groups. Those who have poor self esteem or that come from abusive backgrounds are a prime target for recruitment. Satanism is a religion based upon power, fear is the primary tool used to motivate its members. Our God does not give us the spirit of fear; God does give us a sound mind, authority and love. The gods of the cults invoke fear into their worshippers. They demand worship, not out of love, but out of obedience! It is a system with great uncertainties. They can never be sure if their rituals are going to work properly or if they will backfire. They can never attain a point of having permanent joy. Instead they go from one ritualistic high to the next. The cults are in a religion that often includes the use of drugs, for opening the third eye or to attain different levels of awareness. Another common practice that is common for them is deviant sexual practices, which includes bestiality, sodomy, incest, pedophilia, homosexuality, eating of feces and the drinking of urine, and lesbianism and homosexuality. Abuse is very common from infancy throughout their life span. They mix pain with sadistic pleasure. They replace love with hate and pain for pleasure. The torturing of animals and humans is common. These groups provide a great deal of child pornography and human trafficking. The sexual molestation of the young and innocent are normal practices.

> " And they cause their sons and their daughters to pass through the fire, and used divination and enchantments , and sold themselves to do evil in the sight of the Lord , to provoke him to anger ."[229]

This is a sad reality. All across this country and around the world, there are those, who as a regular part of their pagan rituals use and abuse innocent children. May the Lord have mercy upon them.

The parameters of evil are not limited to nor satisfied with the abuse of humans and animals but often the life of the victim is extinguished. Death row inmate Sean Sellers said that after torturing, killing and cutting up his first animal the transition to killing humans was, not only easy, but incredibly enjoyable! The drinking of blood in the occult is very common and often includes cannibalism. It is a religion of indulgence. The weak are to be used by the strong, however they see fit. Any counselor working with someone coming out of the cult should be very cautious. Seek the leading of God at every point, as there will be a great deal of deception involved. Many who have suffered at the hands of a cult, will have had a great deal of the Bible taught to them, in perverted and twisted ways, to accommodate the desires of the cult. God has called us to preach the gospel to all living beings. This includes those in the cults. Let us go forth, carrying Jehovahnissi, Christ our banner, and trust the heavenly Father to draw them to salvation. They do not need the unholy spirits of this world, these people are slaves in the darkness. They need the life giving, indwelling of the Holy

---

[229] 2 Kings 17:17

Spirit. They need to be set free and to experience the healing, peace and the joy of the Spirit.[230]

Now that you know all of this; what are some of the problems you can expect working with those coming out of the cult? First of all you must beware of the game. They will try to set you; just like the woman I mentioned before was sent to have an affair with me. Many a good man or woman of God has been set up, to fall into some type of sin by those in the cult. I remember a woman that would bake things for me and then bring them to my office. She would call me at the church office wanting to talk about nightmares that were driving her crazy. She would try to expound on these dreams but they were very sexual in nature. Her goal was to tell them to me in order to arouse me. I would not allow her to tell me them but recommended she discuss them with her husband. Another ploy of hers was that she would try to get me alone by visiting me, when my wife would be gone. She would show up unexpectedly at the church so I would immediately leave the building as I called my wife. I would tell her that she could not show up to the church alone but she would always have an excuse. I would keep my wife on the phone until I could get out of the building, so as to protect my testimony. These people will try to pass demons of lust into a person in order to lead them into sexual sin or to open doorways for demons of fear or other vices to come into.

---

[230] Exodus 17:15

Here is sound advice: Never let a client go into any details about any sexual experience or deviant practices. You need to keep your thoughts and mind clean. There is a saying, curiosity kills the cat. This means that even if you are curious fight the urge; do not listen to anything filthy. It will poison your mind. If the person must confess something then leave the room and let them confess it to the Lord privately.

Another way that counselors have been set up is by a person programmed to commit suicide when you go to counsel them. This is an extreme measure but it is one that I personally experienced. I had a person come to me for counsel who was programmed to trigger when I prayed at the beginning of the session. I always open my sessions with prayer. I do not pray with my eyes closed because I have seen far too many people react from the power of prayer. As soon as I said the name of the Father this person immediately grabbed their purse pulling out a piece of glass that was at least seven inches in length and then tried to commit suicide. Praise God my prayer partner grabbed her arm before she could kill herself. The Trigger was designed so that when I prayed she was to kill herself in my office. Her *"family"* would then sue the church. They were through using her and saw this as a means to get rid of her, making a profit, shutting the church doors, and putting me out of the ministry. This person was SRA-DID and had been programmed to react through hypnotism.[231] I removed the triggers and the program and then worked with; at least seven alternate personalities that day, before organizing the internal systems of the various levels of her

---

[231] See my book on this subject called, ─The Big Book on Dissociate Identity Disorder

conscious. I asked this person how they had heard of me and they did not know. I asked them who had referred them to me they and they could not remember that either. They just knew they were to come to me for counseling. They had called me two days prior to see if I had the time to see them and then they drove 5 ½ hours from another state for the appointment. Beware of who you counsel. It may not be God's will for you to counsel every person that comes to you. You must seek the Lord's direction at each point.

Another way that cultists play the game is with those whom are considered piers. Many in the cult have been raised for specific job placement. In the counseling field you will find those, who portray themselves as believers and Christian counselors but all the while they are still heavily dedicated to the cult. These counselors will reinforce programming in the clients that come to them.

Let me restate this: Instead of taking out the programming they will reinforce it. To be quite honest the networking of those in the occult is beyond imagination. They have infiltrated all levels of society including the fields of social work, church pastorates, and counseling centers. They will continue the programming and abuse. These false associates will ask if they can have permission to pray for you. Be very careful who you give permission to pray for you. If they get this authority, they may use it against you in a ritual later. This can be a very powerful legal doorway that they can use against you later.

Another form of attack is in the areas of finance and testimony. The cult will target your finances and ability to pay your bills by cursing you to lose their job or to have their finances devoured. They will seek to ruin your marriage by doing things to make your spouse jealous or to bring division into the marriage so they can hinder the prayers of the husband. They will curse your children, in any way that they can, to tear apart the family unit. They will seek to ruin your testimony by gossip and spreading lies about you and your family. They will try to lead the individual family members into sin. Your children will directly be targeted. They will assign kids from cult families to be cruel to your children by harassing them and beating them up. They will also assign different children, to then befriend your child so they can establish bonds of friendship with them and then use these children to draw yours into the cult.

The greatest victory they can have against a counselor it to convert their children to the cult. What is not commonly known is that all Satanists are required to join Bible believing, Bible preaching churches, in order to destroy it from the inside. The worm destroys the apple by eating away at it, from the inside out. These are just a few areas to be considered. We must be sober and vigilant, for our enemy is very deceptive and will use any way possible, to destroy the work of the Lord.

A Basic Guideline Of Spirits . . .

Spirits are all around us. The world is full of spirits of every type and sort. Let me explain; I use the term spirits as a general term for the fallen angels, which are commonly referred to as demons. In the gospels when it speaks about our Lord casting our demons, the word that is used is *pneuma* which means a spirit. Like the wind is a somewhat intangible element it does have substance and it certainly has power to effect change. All you have to do is look at the after math of a hurricane or tornado to understand the destructive force of the wind. Wind is the movement of air. The spirit is likened to the movement of the breath; it is that which give life to the body. The simple act of breathing moves wasted gases out of our bloodstream and re-energizes our blood through imparting the oxygen needed to live and thrive. Spirits are the angelic entities that are responsible for maintaining and regulating all of the cosmos. The ancient druids believed that every blade of grass, every living thing and even the rocks and hills had spirits that were assigned over them to control and regulate them. This is based upon the truth of the creation of God. When God created the universe, he made Adam the care taker over the earth and its many different facets. God made angels to be the ministering spirits that Adam and his children would use to control and regulate the creation.[232] Spirits are angels that are elemental in nature. They are designed to control the elements. For a better understanding, on the

---
[232] Hebrews 1:14

nature and position of angels I would like to refer you to a book I wrote on the subject called; "The Beast Within." I delves very deeply into the position and influence of angels and their relation to man.

In spiritual warfare counseling you are going to have many clients with spiritual problems. The roots of many of these problems will stem from the spirits of the world. This is why it is important to understand how we are to face these unseen challenges. Notice the following:

" Put on the whole amour of God, that ye may be able to stand against the wiles of the devil. For we wrestle not against flesh and blood, but against *principalities, against powers, against the rulers of the darkness of this world, against spiritual wickedness in high places*. Wherefore take unto you the whole armor of God, that ye may be able to withstand in the evil day, and having done all, to stand."[233]

Notice first of all that we are to put on the armor of God to stand against the *wiles* of the Devil. The word wiles is *methodia*, and it means the method of the Devil. He has a method of how he works against us. The actual definition of method includes the way that the devil works in his plans and schemes but it even goes into more depth in that it identifies the motivation of the teachings assocaiated with the devil. The reason why we need to put on the armor of God is because the Devil will attack us in a spiritual manner. As you saw earlier in the chapter on the armor of God, putting on the armor

---

[233] Ephesians 6:11-13

involves a declaration of what God has done for us and then resting in the work of the Lord, trusting in His power. It is the power of God that keeps us secure in Christ.[234] The Devil will try to wrestle against our faith and commitment unto God. It is his desire to entrap us in sin and despair to make us ineffectual for the Kingdom of God. The Devil and all of the angels were created by Jesus Christ and for Jesus Christ.

> "For by him, (Jesus Christ), were all things created , that are in heaven, and that are in earth , visible and invisible , whether they be ***thrones , or dominions , or principalities , or powers*** : all things were created by him and for him: " [235]

In this verse are listed four specific angelic positions that orchestrate the methods of the Devil.

First let's examine the Devil and then I will briefly cover some of theother spirits listed in the Scriptures. There is an entity that is the Devil that leads all the other spirits of this world. He has many spirits that are called devils, because they do his will. They are little versions of him that ensure that his work is being carried out.

    1) The Devil:

---

[234] 1 Peter 1:5
[235] Colossians 1:16

a. "The devil is the head of the array of fallen angelic forces that were cast down from heaven for following the rebellion of the head angel Lucifer, who wanted to be like the true God.

b. The devils work corporately in opposition to all of the will of God under the leadership of the Devil. They are seeking to destroy all that is good and wholesome to life and liberty.

c. Devils are completely dark and negative. They suck the life from everything they influence. Those heavily influenced by devils, will often feel drained and tired. They will have lives that are filled with stress. The devils are like a pack of wolves that relentlessly pursue and assault the children of God.

d. Devils are devious and diabolical; the word diabolical actually finds its roots in the word devil. They are continually scheming in how they can control, possess and destroy mankind, who are the image bearers of God.

e. The word devil is actually the early English word to do evil. It speaks of rebellion or self will, which is the sin of witchcraft. Witchcraft is choosing your own way over God's will for your life. In the early English to do evil was the word, d'evil, the word we use for devil.

f. There is a battle of good versus evil happening between the obedient angels of God that work to carry out the will of God in His creation and the fallen angels of Lucifer that are now the demons of this world. The evil angels seek to destroy the works of God and to hinder the fulfilling of His promises to his children and his decreed will over creation. In the human realm it is spiritual warfare. It is fallen angels that are seeking to control and influence the person's spirit for destruction.

1) Principalities:[236]
    a. A principality is an entity that has pre-eminence, rule, and authority over all the other angels in his area of influence.[237]
    b. Principalities rule over terrestrial regions of the earth commanding all the angels in that area. They often will inhabit the person who has the most influence in that area, using it as a throne from which they will rule. An example of a principality is found in Daniel chapter ten. In this account a powerful angelic messenger has been sent from the true God to answer the prayers of Daniel but the principality of Persia, had withstood the angelic messenger for twenty one days, until God sent Michael, a arch angel to help his original messenger get to Daniel. After delivering the message, the angel tells Daniel that he must return to fight with the principality of Persia and that after he has left, the principality of Greece would next come to contend with Daniel.[238] In this account we see the war between God's angels of light and the satanic principalities of darkness.
2) Powers:[239]
    a. Powers are spirits that have authority over:
        i. Individuals; specifically those in powerful positions or positions of influence. They also will take a position of influential power over a family's line, claiming authority over the children and children's-children continuing their rule, for sometimes thousands of generations until the spirit of sin and the generational curses are destroyed.

---

[236] Jeremiah 13:18; Romans 8:38; Ephesians 1:21,3:10, 6:12; Colossians 1:16, 2:10, 2:15; Titus 3:1
[237] Daniel 10:13,20-21, 12:1; Matthew 9:34, 12:24, 20:25; John 12:31,14:30, 16:11; 1 Corinthians 2:6,8; Ephesians 2:2
[238] Daniel 10:10-20
[239] Ephesians 6:12

ii. Over regions: Powers can place coverings of darkness and evil over areas that have been dedicated to them through formal ceremonies, acts of worship, or heathen-idolatrous practices. Areas of land where a great evil has happened are given invitation and authority for a Power to establish its dark covering. It will use the area to work from, increasing its span of influence as it spreads out its cloak of darkness over the region. Over the centuries, many historians have written of darkness that comes upon an area of land where a great evil has happened. They say that the evil can be felt in the air, like some dark, ominous presence. The darkness then spreads to the land, draining the life from everything. The land eventually becomes desolate, dry and filled with thorns and briers. This covering of evil can cover vast amounts of land, even whole regions.[240]

iii. Businesses: Some businesses are of particular interest to the kingdom of darkness for their ability to impact many different levels of society. A business can be greatly used in extending demonic influence. Many of these businesses are shrouded in humanitarian covers. Some of the most evil are considered the most philanthropic of society. They are a beautiful side of evil; the worst kind because they promote just causes for humanity. They often will be generous in giving to the needy or causes of good. In order to delay judgment they will do a certain amount of what is considered good. This is because their agenda is to create unholy alliances by unequally yoking themselves to the

---

[240] Psalm 44:19; Isaiah 34:13, 35:7 (for a reversal of the cursed land); Jeremiah 9:11, 10:22, 49:33, 51:37; Malachi 1:3

unwary. This unholy union gives them the authority they need, to influence the decision making abilities, of all those associated with the business. Many, many ministries have been destroyed by accepting money from evil people or organizations. Remember that Abraham would not take anything from the evil kings, not even a shoe string. He did not want them to be associated with him in any way. His dependence was upon the true God; not man.[241] This is just one of the many ways a business comes under the influence of a king of darkness. A *Power* will enter into an agreement with those who have authority over the business. Those on the receiving end of the agreement rarely know that they have been brought into a relationship, with a king of darkness. By choosing a philosophy of conduct, that goes against the revealed will, of the true God, the persons business is automatically placed under the authority of the kingdom of darkness. The power will place its covering over the person's mind and heart. It will then begin to spread a veil of darkness over the entire business. The dark covering of the business will taint and affect every person that it comes in contact with it. This is the reason that the Bible teaches that we are to offer everything we have and receive, to the true God in prayer, giving Him praise for it and then asking for his blessing upon the items we buy.[242] The owners of the business do not have to

---

[241] Genesis 14:21-24
[242] Job 34:4; Romans 14:14; 2 Corinthians 6:14-18; 1 Thessalonians 5:18; 1 Timothy 4:3-4

do an actual ceremony,[243] or engage in an agreement that acknowledges, the power or the kingdom of darkness to be under its influence. It can happen in pure ignorance of the spiritual laws. If a person or business conducts itself according to anti-Biblical principles, it is already working under and for the kingdom of darkness. Let me state it another way: All that needs to take place, for the Power to establish its position of authority over a business, is for the owners, or those in the positions of authority in the business, to give themselves over to the leading of a devil. Again let me state this clearly: By rejecting God's holy principles and standards for business declared in the Bible, the business is automatically given over to witchcraft through default.[244] Because the world and its philosophies are against the word of God, many business practices that violate God's word are considered ethical and morally right in societal practice. Just because the world say's it's ok to do something; it does not make it right. No matter how philosophically right something may appear to be, if it contradicts the word of God, than it is of the kingdom of darkness, and for this cause alone; a Power has the right to rule over it. On the other hand if a business is intentionally given over to the true God, setting its order of practice according to God's revealed word, it will have the protective hand of God

---

[243] Some businesses are intentionally given over to the kingdom of darkness. I have worked with 100's of occultists who have given me vivid descriptions of the preparations they have gone through in order to prepare for lavish ceremonies of demonic empowering and dedication to specific entities in order to have the power and influence of a prince of darkness in their business. These ceremonies specifically seek to influence all they touch.

[244] Witchcraft is choosing your own way over God's revealed will. It is the sin of rebellion. Rebellion, though often subtle gives a power authority over the business.

upon it, along with His Holy Spirit leading and guiding those involved. It will also become a source of influence to everyone that it touches.[245]

    iv. A power is a powerful devil that has the ability to place a dark covering over someone or something. This authority will influence all of the decision making abilities of everything under its covering for the kingdom of darkness.[246] They will manipulate thoughts, emotions and actions. This is illustrated in the veil covering the head of a married woman. It was a symbolic gesture showing that she was married and under the authority of her husband.[247] It was a sign of respect for her husband telling others that he was her spokesperson in the congregation.[248] When an angelic entity places its dark veil over something, it symbolizes its power and authority over it. As previously stated the dark covering can be over a person, family line, territory or business.

3) There are three Hebrew words for devil. One that is used in the Scriptures is the word "***shed***." This is where we get the term shade from.[249] The word shade literally means that which tries to intercept the rays of the sun, in order to keep the person from receiving the light of the Sun. It is a dark covering. When the Bible uses the word shed for devil, it is describing the purpose of the shade. The shade is a creature whose sole design is to stand between God and his

---

[245] Psalm 34:7; Matthew 6:13; Luke 11:4; Romans 15:7; 1 Corinthians 10:31; 2 Corinthians 4:15
[246] There are good, elect angels that watch over God's children allowing for the power of the Holy Spirit to lead, influence and guide in a way that honors God and brings Him glory.
[247] I Corinthians 11:10
[248] I Corinthians 14:34; 1 Timothy 2:12
[249] Deuteronomy 32:17; Psalm 106:37

people; to keep them from worshipping God and receiving his blessings and power for their life. The shade is a creature of the darkness. When it is assigned to a person, it becomes a dark covering over them. This covers them with the power of the kingdom of darkness. Darkness is void of all light. I have worked with many individuals coming out of the occult and they have told me how there are several rituals they use to summon and place shades over their children and grandchildren so they will never be able to hear the truth of salvation. They intentionally condemn their children as an offering to the kingdom of darkness. Jesus Christ is the light of the world, the darkness cannot take him in; the shade can only *try* to stand between you and your God. The shade can only try to sever you from the power of God in your life.[250] The only way this can be accomplished is by you giving yourself over to habitual sin. The shade uses the method of diversion. It will tempt you by a sin of some sort to try to get you to take your eyes off the Lord. The shade will try to get your focus on anything other than the true Lord Jesus Christ. If he can do this he can separate you from the power of God in your life. He can never separate you from the love of God;[251] when you are in Christ you are eternally secure but the Bible is very clear; if you give yourself over to a sin, than God will restrain his hand of power in your life, until you turn back to him in repentance. The shade will try to lead you further and further into sin, until you have committed the sin unto death.[252] The sin unto death is a phrase that indicates that there is a point a person can cross where God will take him home to heaven. Only God knows what the point of no return is for the believer. But since you are God's possession, when you are no longer able to serve him upon this earth because of a heart hardened by sin, God will call

---

[250] John 8:12, 1:5: Isaiah 59:1-3; Romans 1:28
[251] Romans 8:39
[252] Ezekiel 3, 33; Acts 20:17-26; Romans 6:16; 1 John 5:16

you home to be with him. You do not lose your salvation; you simple are called home to live with the Father in heaven. You are an ambassador of Christ.[253] It is your life that is to be a witness of the great God we serve. When you cease to be that ambassador God will call you home to be with him. A shade will try to remove you from the war for the souls of men and woman. A shade will lead you into sin and then he will develop that sin until it has become a demonic stronghold.[254] This is spiritual warfare! A stronghold is when a person feels helpless and hopeless to be free from a particular sin, habit, circumstance or situation they are in. Jesus is the hope of the world.[255] The shade cannot create a stronghold in a person that is holding onto this truth!

4) Rulers of the darkness of this world
   a. Rulers of darkness are literally: *Kosmokrator skotos*: meaning that there are a group of angels that are rulers over the darkness of this world. The darkness of this world is the practices, places and inhabitants that are separated from the light of Jesus Christ. These Rulers oversee, the Powers that are the coverings over these practices, places and inhabitants. The rulers of darkness dictate, govern and formulate the plans, on how the kingdom of darkness is to spread its area of affect and control. The ruler is the demonic angel that knows the bigger picture of Satan's plans. It is his job to ensure that all under his command are working together to bring about the completion of the greater agenda. The power is under the command of the Ruler.
   b. The primary effect of darkness is to separate people, places and items from the influence and power of God's Holy Spirit. They seek to mask

---

[253] Ephesian 6:20; 2 Corinthians 5:20
[254] 1 John 2:16; James 1:14; Ephesians 4:26-27; 2 Corinthians 10:4
[255] Psalm 22:9

the truth about man's position and place, in the scheme of God. They seek to blind men to the truth of their condition, hindering their ability to acknowledge their need for salvation.[256] They manipulate and bend the will of the unregenerate, with deceit, lies and trickery.[257] The Rulers command where the dark powers are to concentrate their efforts for spreading their dark coverings.

c. One important thing to note is this: Rulers also can take a position over the heart of an individual. When a heart has been shattered and broken and is filled with pain, bitterness and hatred it is an open doorway for a person to be given over/enslaved to darkness. This is how the Devil, that goes about as a roaring lion devours its prey. It swallows the broken and torn individual; totally surrounding them in darkness. Like Jonah who was in the belly of the beast, suffering horribly and being tortured by the inside of the stomach of the great fish; these poor souls are trapped in a world of darkness. They believe they are hopeless and helpless. Their minds and hearts have been shattered. They are the perfect place for a ruler of darkness to reside.

d. A Ruler of darkness can work through an individual that has been deeply wounded. If it can establish a dark throne in the person, it will be able to use that person to bring about greater works for the kingdom of darkness. It would not be uncommon for a Ruler of darkness to work in the hearts and mind of a parent so they can control the nurturing of the child. They will use family lines to create children tailored for work in the kingdom of darkness. Time is on their side. They work towards the greater goal of the kingdom of darkness.

---

[256] 1 Corinthians 2:14
[257] Ephesians 2:1-3

e. One example, of how a Ruler of darkness uses a person's heart is in the field of mind control programming. The dark throne in the programmer will enable them, to without mercy, guilt or remorse, shatter the minds of small children and infants through trauma based pain and torture. The ability to control the person through hypnotism is also a gift of the dark ruler. If the person has an unholy tie or attachment the dark ruler can control the mind of the abused giving the abuser/programmer complete control over the persons mind, will and emotional regulation. When the abuser shatters the individuals mind, the power of darkness takes authority over the broken shards of the psyche placing powers of darkness, over each of the splits.[258] These entities keep the parts/ alternate personalities, separated and enslaved. When a child's heart had been broken, powers of darkness will cover the individual pieces. This will keep the person in a state of being continually separated, leaving them feeling forever bound in a state of helplessness and hopelessness. They will remain in this state until someone that is lead by the Holy Spirit takes the time to help them out of the darkness. The Ruler of darkness ensures that the job of separating the child's mind is complete, placing a dark covering over each of the separate pieces. A heart that is torn apart and covered in darkness is the perfect place a dark throne to rule from. When a heart is shattered and then separated, theoretically, it is unable, wholeheartedly search for the true God.[259] The plan is to prevent the person from ever obtaining true freedom and deliverance. It is the cruelest and most diabolical form of abuse there is. The person with the ruler of darkness in them will work to completely enslave the

---

[258] Splits is the term used for creating alternate personalities as in dissociative identity disorder
[259] Jeremiah 29:13

heart, mind, soul and spirit of others through abuse and trauma. The goal is to never allow them to feel love. They replace love with hatred, joy with pain and peace with bitterness. They plant seeds of hatred for others, themselves and God within their heart. Blaming God and everyone else for the abuse they have suffered. The Rulers of darkness work in some of the following ways:

i. By rendering people spiritually blind to the things of the true God.[260]

ii. They keep people ignorant of the divine things of God this includes human duty and responsibilities to Him. A life ignorant of the divine will of God will result in ungodliness and immorality, eventually leading to consequent misery in hell for all eternity.

iii. Rulers take control of a person's thoughts, their mind and their emotions. They work to bring the person completely under the command of the dark ruler over them. They do not work by plaguing the person's mind with blatantly evil thoughts. What they do is mix truth and lies together, attaching them to the person's emotions. They will harden the person's heart through lies and deceit until the person is no longer sensitive to the difference between wrong and right. When a person has lost the ability to know wrong from right they are a reprobate.[261] These individuals will often be incredibly devoted to a particular form of religion or a greater cause of good. They are trapped in the *beautiful* side of evil. Often they will take part in philanthropically engineered organizations. Money, power, and

---
[260] John 12:40; Romans 11:7; 2 Corinthians 3:14, 4:4; 1 John 2:11
[261] Jeremiah 6:30; Romans 1:28; 2 Timothy 3:8; Titus 1:16

position are some of the tools they use to further their influence. The world's definition of success is very different than the Bible's. A person with a ruler of darkness in them will often live a very wholesome and good life. This appearance of living right gives them a greater amount of influence to use for destroying lives and further spreading the powers of darkness.[262]

5) Spiritual wickedness in high places
   a. Spiritual wickedness results from pervasive idolatry. Spiritual Wickedness in High Places is a demonic entity that rules over those that are given over, to pervasive idolatry. Churches all over the world are havens of spiritual wickedness! These religious rulers of the heart, enslave and damn entire groups and civilizations. If it were not for the power of God's election, none would be saved from their damnable effect. These are very powerful entities that inhabit all false religious leaders. They can be found in Christian pulpits and in satanic covens. They work through the spirit of the person, rather than the intellect. Rather than expounding the truth of God's word, these leaders under the control of a wicked spirit will, will water down the Word of God or they will leave it out of their message altogether. A dear friend brought it to my attention that the mega-churches of today no longer preach the word of God in its entirety; rather they just give the *"cliff note"* version. We need all of the council of God to live a life that is surrendered to God. These entities will tickle your ears and touch your heart with *good spiritual experiences* of praise and worship, all the

---

[262] Ephesians 2:1-3

while leading you into damnation.[263] They replace truth with emotions. These angels of spiritual wickedness, assign the rulers of darkness over individuals, groups, denominations and organizations, which in turn, distribute the angelic powers of darkness amongst the members. They work in unison with the principalities over regions, but are in rank and position over principalities. I have talked with many Satanists that told me they were assigned to churches in order to infiltrate and destroy it from within. They said they would feign salvation and then ask to get baptized. This would make them a member of the church. Once they were a member of the church, since they were also a Satanist, it gave the entire coven of cultist the authority to curse, hex and vex the members. Spiritual warfare is real; so is the effect of fallen angels.

b. These religious spirits work to draw devotion and worship away from the true God unto themselves.[264] They seek to blind and mislead mankind, keeping them from the truth of God's word. They stir up spirits of animosity against the truth of God's word. They seek to lead mankind into rebellion against the Lord God and His Christ. This is the core of Luciferian worship. These spirits seek to dethrone God offering the throne of Satan or Lucifer instead. They make them children of the beast; i.e. children of the damned.[265] When a person comes under the control, of a ruler of spiritual wickedness in high places, it is because they have placed themselves under the mark of the beast.[266] The mark of the beast is the internal surrendering to the ruling of the god of this world, and the committing to the philosophy of life.

---

[263] Matthew 7:13; 2 Timothy 2:16, 3:1-9; Jude
[264] Deuteronomy 16:18-22; Psalm 146:8
[265] Isaiah 14; Ezekiel 28; Deuteronomy 6:4-9; Revelations 13:16-17, 14:9,11, 15:2, 16:2, 19:20, **20:4**
[266] Deuteronomy 6:4-9 shows God's mark upon an individual. Revelations 16:2, 19:20

It is a rejection of the truth of God and an acceptance of the god of this world with an embracing of the sin of rebellion.

c. These spirits rule over those that refuse to give God control over their hearts, minds, souls and spirits. They are over those that self-willed.[267]

d. Those under the effect of these entities will trade true devotion and worship, with an adherence to the literal authority of the Scriptures, for a religion that makes them feel sincere and safe. There will be no fear of, or reverence of the true God. They will have no fear of condemnation nor a belief in the literalness of hell.

e. You can identify those under the spell of these spirits by clear and evident signs. For instance, they will often equate their devotion to God by their worship experience; i.e., their feelings and emotions rather than the truths conveyed in the word of God. They have a subjective form of worship; with a what's in it for me mentality. Does it make me feel good?

f. I remember an incident that changed my understanding about Christian service. I was in my first year of Bible College and had gotten very excited about the prospects of Pastoring so I approached an individual that I respected and expressed the possibility of being called to a small church. He turned to me and said that he would never consider a church of less than 400 members, as he had to have a large salary to support his lifestyle. He was in the ministry for the money, not the calling. These religious entities control churches, denominations and

---

[267] Job 41:31

even countries. They are the epitome of the spirit of the anti-Christ and as a false-Christ,[268] they are leading all of their followers into hell.

6) Thrones[269]
   a. Thrones are a ruling class of angels. They are typified as having four cherubim positioned at the four corners of their throne, supporting and carrying it where ever the throne wills. They are also surrounded by a large number of seraphim which are under their command.
   b. The title throne signifies that they have a royal throne from which they rule from. This puts them into the ruling class of angels.
   c. The Throne sits enthroned, over the hearts of kings, princes, dictators and rulers, which Satan personally places in positions of power over various kingdoms of the earth.[270] They place their throne over the heart of the individual and sit as a false Christ within them controlling all of their thoughts, emotions and decisions.

7) Dominions[271]
   a. Dominions are lesser entities that seek to take possession of individuals. Hence the word dominion, they dominate. They do not often succeed in taking control of a person, but when they do, they create a demonic stronghold, which affects every aspect of the person.[272] It becomes ground given over to the devil, affecting the person's emotions and their ability to regulate them. While under the control of a demonic stronghold, the individual's ability to make godly decisions will be askew.

---

[268] Anti Christ means a pseudo Christ or one just like. The word Christ speaks of the anointed one of God, who could lead and deliver those who follow Him.
[269] Colossians 1:16
[270] Daniel 7:9; Matthew 4:8-9; Luke 4:5-7; Colossians 1:16; Revelations 2:13, 13:2, 16:10
[271] Colossians 1:16
[272] Ephesians 4:30

b. A person does not always have obvious signs when under the control of a dominion. The dominion will not seek to draw attention to itself. It will create and control a spiritual stronghold that will house a variety of lesser spirits.[273] These spirits will often reveal themselves in emotional regulation issues and compulsive sin patterns. A person with a dominion will have a chaotic life. The stronghold is identified by feelings of helplessness and hopelessness. Some examples of spiritual strongholds are gluttony, smoking, fear, anxiety, etc. You can identify the spirits in a stronghold by this: Whatever the sin problem is, that will be the name of the demonic spirit in the stronghold of the dominion.

c. These entities can only have control over someone if the person gives it to them. By giving themselves over to the sin, they allow a dominion to come in gain control.[274] A curse or cursed object can also allow the entrance of a dominion into a person.

d. Demonic strongholds are the result of an inhabiting dominion. The dominion holds the stronghold, not revealing itself, but allowing other sinful spirits to do their work in controlling various aspects of the person. Like a person that owns a hotel can give rooms to whoever they choose; a dominion that has gained ground in an individual can invite in other spirits to stay in the ground they have gained.

e. Demonic possession results when the dominion takes complete control over the person. One example would be the person who was unable to speak because of a demonic possession.[275] The Scriptures have many

---

[273] Luke 11:17-26; 2 Corinthians 10:4
[274] Isaiah 59:1-3
[275] Matthew 9:33, 10:8, 12:28; Mark 1:34, 39, 3:15, 16:17; Luke 11:20, 13:32

references to demonic spirits, i.e. fallen angels being cast out of individuals."[276]-[277]

There is a great deal of organization in the spirit realm. The very nature and design of an angel is to control and keep order within creation so naturally in the kingdom of darkness there is a well organized system of order. The best way to describe the spiritual realm of angels is in the illustration of an army. The satanic army consists of spirit with varying ranks, strengths and abilities. Each and every aspect of the spiritual military has an appointed place of service. Like a finely woven tapestry, with each of the spirits being a thread; if you were to see the picture from the God's viewpoint you would see a complete picture. It may seem like the world is in chaos but actually everything the Devil is doing, is working for the completion of God. God is the Great Designer and He has made everything for His own purpose. This includes the fallen angels. Though they work against God and his kingdom, they fulfill the will of God. I had a man explain it to me like this once.

He said; the devil is like an evil man that hated a person who owned a apple orchard. One day the evil man said I'm going to do something that hurts my neighbor, I'm going to chop down his favorite tree; that will show him. That night the evil man went and chopped down the huge apple tree but when it fell it pinned him to the ground. The next day the owner of the apple orchard came out with another man and found him. The evil man laughed

---

[276] The Beast Within; Dr. Tom Knotts, Jr. pg.'s 10-11
[277] Psalm 34:7; Matthew 6:13; Luke 11:4; Romans 15:7; 1 Corinthians 10:31; 2 Corinthians 4:15

and said, I may be hurt but I killed your favorite apple tree. The orchard owner replied I was bringing this lumber man here to remove this tree so I could build a home. I was going to use the wood from this tree to build my house. You thought evil against me but actually you have saved me time and money by doing the work for me. The devil works against God and his children but in actuality God has already planned how everything will work out. He already included everything the devil and his minions will do in the plan, so in essence, in their rebellion they are completing the will of God.

All angels are ministering spirits to God's children

> "But to which of the angels said he at any time, Sit on my right hand, until I make thine enemies thy footstool? Are they not all ministering spirits, sent forth to minister for them who shall be heirs of salvation?"[278]

We know of a certainty that God does not tempt anybody with evil, neither can He be tempted with evil,[279] but God does allow things to happen in his providential plan that often would appear to be cruel or destructive to his child. This is because He has a wonderful plan for each and every one of His children. Sometimes that plan may include great sorrow and suffering. We see right now darkly, like the person behind the tapestry cannot see the

---

[278] Hebrews 1:13-14
[279] James 1:13-14

beautiful picture that is displayed in the front, but the day will come when all will be revealed. Our God is perfect, He makes no mistakes and we can trust fully in His providential care. Imagine how Job must have felt, losing his children, having his body wracked with pain, as boils and oozing sores covered him and then having all his possessions taken; his herds and livestock and fields.[280] If that weren't enough his own wife turns against him and tells him to curse God and die.[281] Then Job gets to enjoy the visit of his three friends, who also accuse him of sin and belittle him. From the view of all those around Job, it appeared that God had turned against him, but actually the opposite was happening. God the Father was keeping Satan and his minions on a leash restricting them from what they would like to actually do, only allowing what He knew Job would be able to handle. Our God will not allow us to experience more than we can handle but will with each and every temptation or trial, He will make a way of escape.[282] This is a term which means that the captain of the ship will throw over board that which will sink the vessel. In all actuality, the trials that assailed Job were an answer to his prayer. Job wanted to see God.[283] It would be through this great trial that Job would grow, not only in the knowledge of the Lord, but also he would get to see God and talk with him, face to face.[284] God in the end blessed Job more than He had before the trial. The Bible is true when it states . . .

---

[280] Job 1:12-22
[281] Job 2:9
[282] 1 Corinthians 10:13
[283] Job 19:26
[284] Job 42:25

> "And we know that all things work together for good to them that love God , to them who are the called according to his purpose."[285]

All angels are ministering spirits to those who are heirs to salvation; this includes the fallen ones also. They know who the children in heaven are and they know who the children of God are, upon the earth. Demonic spirits must have permission from God to do anything to one of God's children. You do not raise your hand against a prince or princess, without invoking the fury of the King. It is important that as believer's in Christ, we understand that the fallen angels have already been defeated. They were openly declared defeated in the streets of heaven. They were stripped of any ability they once had. They have to have permission to do anything.

> "And having spoiled principalities and powers, he made a shew of them openly , triumphing over them in it ."[286]

The fallen angels know whether you are a child of God or not. The Scriptures tell us that greater is He that is in you than he that is in the world.[287] This is speaking about the Holy Spirit abiding in us. The demonic realm can see this. They know if you are a child of God and they also know they have to obey you when you command them. They will try to lead you

---
[285] Romans 8:28
[286] Colossians 2:15
[287] 1 John 4:4

into sin and they will work at trying to separate you from the will of God but they cannot force a child of God to do anything. If you fall into sin, it is your decision to do so and you will suffer the consequences for what you do. If you sow the wind you will reap a tornado.[288] Sin costs more than you really want to pay and demons will try to take you for everything you have. They will seek to destroy your life and the life of all those around you. On top of this God has made sure that every angel in heaven and earth knows who his children are.

"For this cause I bow my knees unto the Father of our Lord Jesus Christ, Of whom the whole family in heaven and earth is named."[289]

I learned about the authority of God first hand. It was during an encounter with a incubus that this became all too real for me. An individual came to my office and asked to pray for them, so I did. As soon as I prayed for the Father to bind the principalities, she came under extreme physical attack. Her chair was lifted into the air and she was being struck so hard that I could see the impressions of some force sinking into her face and body. She cried out screaming for help. I could not see what it was that was attacking her, so I commanded the spirit to be bound and that's when it physically manifested in front of me. The following is what happened next. "I command you in the name of the Lord Jesus Christ to turn loose of her."

---

[288] Hosea 8:7; Galatians 6:7
[289] Ephesians 3:14-15

Her body was in the air flailing from the physical blows that she was receiving. It did not stop so I cried out, "Father send in warring angels to grab this thing." It was at this point that it stopped hitting her and turned on me. "CAN'T YOU SEE IT!" Her screams were pathetic, I felt so helpless. *"No I can't,"* I responded, but this is when I did get to see it! It manifested right in front of me. It was black with burning red eyes. It had a dragon like body with long claws. Though it was only about 14 inches high; it was terrifying to look at and to be honest I was scared. I said, "You can't hit me, I have the shield of faith." "You have no faith, it hissed, you're only wearing the armor." It was right I thought I was going to die, I was incredibly scarred of it! I lifted my hands in the air and asked God to forgive me for being so afraid of this thing and then asked him to surround me with the shield of faith. I then asked it if I had the shield of faith now and it said I did. I commanded it to tell me why it hadn't did not attack me and it responded, "I don't have permission."

It was during this encounter I learned that a spirit must have permission or legal right to assault a child of God. I also learned that the spiritual creatures can see the armor of God, because it is a spiritual armor. Entities will try to instill in us with the spirit of fear and to make us believe that they are going to destroy us, but they are limited by God the Father and cannot do anything unless He gives them permission. There will be times when God allows the enemy to afflict and strike us down, but that will only happen if it brings glory to God and makes us more like Jesus.[290] The following will be a simple teaching on various spirits in the fallen realm of angels.

We battle not against flesh and blood but against principalities, etc. The word principality literally means Arch or first in rank and power. In Daniel chapter ten, Daniel was praying and fasting unto God for twenty one day but when the angel came to him he stated . . .

"And, behold, an hand touched me, which set me upon my knees and upon the palms of my hands. And he said unto me , O Daniel , a man greatly beloved , understand the words that I speak unto thee , and stand upright : for unto thee am I now sent . And when he had spoken this word unto me, I stood trembling . Then said he unto me , Fear not , Daniel : for from the first day that thou didst set thine heart to understand , and to chasten thyself before thy God , thy words were heard, and I am come for thy words. But the prince of the kingdom of Persia withstood me one and twenty days : but , lo , Michael , one of the chief princes , came to help me ; and I remained there with the kings of Persia."[291]

The angel, after finishing his mission with Daniel, states that he needed to return to fight with the prince of Persia and that after he left, the prince of

---

[290] Luke 22:31; Job 1:6-12, 2:3-6,
[291] Daniel 10:10-13

Greece would come and set himself against Daniel. Daniel was in a continual state of spiritual warfare. All who seek to live righteously will suffer persecution.[292] All persecution that we suffer is driven by the fallen spirits of this world. There is warfare in the heavens and upon earth. Often we think about angelic warfare as something only in a novel, but the Bible is very clear; there are high ranking angels trying to hinder the Lord from answering the prayers of God's people. Another example of direct angelic warfare was when Michael came to gather the body of Moses. Satan personally withstood him. God's angels always do his will and never try to do anything outside of his will. The battle is the Lord's. Rather than fighting Satan the Scriptures tell us that Michael responded thusly:

"Yet Michael the archangel, when contending with the devil he disputed about the body of Moses, durst not bring against him a railing accusation, but said, The Lord rebuke thee."[293]

The Principality is the arch demon that has a prominent position in which he exercises authority. He is a prince over a specific region or territory. For example, there are principalities over each nation, state, city and province. They are given assignments and have beneath them, legions of minions to carry out their assignments.

---

[292] 2 Timothy 3:12
[293] Jude 9

What every counselor should make a practice of doing before starting any counseling session is to pray unto God the Father, asking him to bind the spirits and to release the power of Holy Spirit of God. Before you pray, have the counselee give you permission to pray for them, in proxy for them with authority. This will give you the ability to renounce on their behalf if they cannot speak or are severely attacked. The following is a prayer given to me from William Schnoebelen of the, "With One Accord Ministry." It is the best prayer I have found on the subject.

"DELIVERANCE PROCEDURE

1) BINDING EVIL BEFORE A MEETING

Praise and worship be to El Elyon, the God of all created beings. For by Him the salvation, and the power, and the Kingdom of our God and the authority of His Christ have come. Hallelujah! The evil deceiver has been defeated because of the Blood of the Lamb. As a Christian, I now give testimony to the authority of Jesus Christ, the Messiah, the Holy One of Israel over this place known as I hind with Jesus' Blood, the wicked spiritual forces of evil including all rulers, authorities and cosmic powers of this dark age who are not of the true Lord Jesus Christ as He sees and numbers them in this place.

By the power of Jesus Christ, all forces of evil within this place are now bound from any and all communication, interplay or interaction between themselves or any other forces of evil. Any and all evil access routes, to or from this place, are now severed as I purify with the Blood of the Lamb the AIR, WATER, GROUND, FIRE, and the FORCES OF NATURE and claim them for Christ Jesus and consecrate them unto Him. I bind the SPIRIT WORLD and its forces by the Blood, the Cross and the Name of .Jesus. I take authority over and send back anything coming from the spirit world against anyone in the process of gathering here and or against any member of their family and/or properties. I now repel and utterly defeat any counter-attack launched after this gathering. In the name of Jesus, I bind any darkness brought into this place of gathering by those who gather. Such darkness is now rendered utterly powerless by the Blood of Christ Jesus, the Light of the world, and cannot communicate, interact or interplay with themselves or any other evil forces. Nor can they influence, harm or inhibit any of those who gather here. I now seal this place of gathering by the Blood of the Lamb shed on the cross of Calvary. I invite with thanksgiving, the full and manifest presence of the Ruach ha Qadosh, the Holy Spirit of God to come and dwell here with all wisdom and knowledge for the glory of God through His Son Jesus Christ, the Holy One of Israel.

In the Name of Christ Jesus, I bind any manifestations during or after these proceedings which are not in our Lord Jesus Christ's perfect will. I pray You, Heavenly Father, In Your Loving-kindness to bring all things to our remembrance which You would have us deal with at this time and we thank You for it.

In the Name of the true Lord Jesus Christ, I take authority over and bind any and all lying and deceitful spirits, vain imaginings, false impressions and counterfeit gifts and signs and wonders as well as the Accuser before the throne and command them to go where Jesus tells them to go by the voice of His Holy Spirit. I also ask you, Father, to loose the Spirit of Truth here today, and the Spirit of Power, of Love and of a Sound Mind! I submit totally unto Your Will, El Elyon, and praise You for Your manifest presence and Your protection of Your children here today, in Jesus mighty Name and for His sake. Amen."[294]

As a counselor it is important to understand that you should not cast any spirits out of an individual unless you have to. The best way to deal with a demonic spirit is to have the person confess the sin that allowed the demon to enter into them and then to renounce the sin, asking God to sever all unholy ties and attachments and to command the spirit to go where he commands it to, by the voice of His holy spirit. When all the legal authority for the demon to be in the person has been removed, the demon will have to leave. If you have to cast it out, than it implies that the demon has the legal right to be there. If it does have legal right to be there than it will come back into the person, bringing seven demons more that are even worse than the first.[295] For example, the Bible is very clear about woman not being pastor's

---

[294] Deliverance Procedure-With One Accord ,І William and Sharon Schnoebelen , One Accord Ministries ; Dubuque, Iowa 52004-0457

[295] Matthew 12:44; Luke 11:24

in the church but many people have believed the Devils lie that woman can be preachers even though it directly goes against the word of God.[296] This creates a stronghold in the person, when they give themselves over to this belief. The entity that enters the person through believing this lie, will often not reveal itself, but the ground for the stronghold will allow other spirits to enter into the person. By believing the lie of the devil that woman can be preachers, when the Bible is very clear that they cannot, if you cast the spirits out of the woman they will each return with seven more each that are worse than themselves. This demonic stronghold will continue to grow affecting the person more and more. It will grow slowly. The person needs to learn the truth of the literal word of God and then agree with it before the stronghold can be broken. People need to confess believing false doctrines and then to ask forgiveness for giving themselves over to it.

NOTE: What needs to happen is this: The person need to confess that they have believed a lie and that contradicted the word of God. They need to admit that this is a sin against God and also a sin against all those around them, because they did not stand up for the Truth of God's Word. Once they have done this they need to ask the Lord to cleanse them from this sin, tearing down the stronghold and severing them from all unholy ties and attachment Next they should ask the Lord to command all the unholy spirits to leave them, by the voice of His Holy Spirit sealing them with His Holy Spirit and filling them in all of their empty places with the fruit of His Holy

---

[296] 1 Timothy 2:12; 1 Corinthians 14:34-36

Spirit. If this is properly done the spirit will not need to be cast out; it will leave on its own.

Sometimes a spirit will need to be cast out. One of these times is if the spirits have been given authority to be in the person by the parents of someone else in the family line. These spirits from dedications will try to stay and must be cast out. Some of these family spirits will only come out by prayer and fasting. They are very stubborn and will refuse to leave. When Christ commands them to leave; they must leave. Just remember this; if the person does not repent of believing the lie that allowed the spirit into them, or has repented and renounced the sin that allowed the spirit into them, then the spirit will return with seven others that are worse than it and the person will be in worse shape than when you started.

What about incubus, succubus, and doppelgangers? If you suspect someone of having a doppelganger, by all means do not confront this! Call on someone with experience in this area! You may very easily be killed if a doppelganger comes forward. They are very powerful and cannot be bound because they are a hybrid of the person's soul and body combined with the spirit. They generally will have the supernatural power of a principality at their disposal. Also with incubus and succubus if you have not worked with them before, do not stir them up. Get someone with experience in this area as they can become very violent and often will physically attack the person. Incubus and succubus are demons of sexual violence and wrath. They will have red eyes and have darkness around them invoking great fear upon the person, subjected to their attack. They are the demons described in Genesis six that had forced themselves upon woman. They come in four basic substance compositions of varying tangibility from immaterial to fully physically manifesting. If one does appear, claim by faith the sword of the spirit and literally stab it until it goes away or backs down. The creature is spiritual and the sword of the spirit will fend it off! Also cry out to God to send in holy angels to physically grab it and to keep it from assaulting you.

Demonic spirits have different appearances. Their eyes tell a great deal about them. Demons with yellow eyes are typically demons of lust or temptation. If the person's eyes turn yellow when confronted than it means they are a nephilim. A nephilim is a angel that is attached at the genetic level. The person was born with the angel in them, from conception. Just like John the Baptist and Samson were born with the Holy Spirit of God in them these people are conceived with the demonic spirits joined to their spirits. Green eyed demons are demons of jealousy, hatred and stubbornness. Red eyed demons are demons of wraith and violence, usually sexual violence. Black eyed demons are demons of death. Just remember no matter what you encounter, the Lord will always answer your call for help, so call on him, asking him to send angels of his choosing, to grab the thing or to simply save and defend you. I have had to do this several times and though there were times I thought I was going to be killed, the Lord has always protected me, His child.

A Short Word On DID . . .

DID means; disassociation identity disorder. When a child, whether male or female, prior to the age of seven is sexually molested or placed in a situation of extreme duress or neglect they will dissociate from the event. Dissociation is a God given ability to mentally escape from the situation causing the trauma. This survival coping mechanism gives the person the ability to keep sane, in situations that would otherwise destroy their mind. DID has varying degrees, from the simple disassociate who has fragmented memories, to the extreme poly-fragmented who may have hundreds or even thousands of alternate personalities, each having varying degrees of substance. The person, who is a dissociate, will usually not know that they have the disorder. This is why you can have client with two very different alternate personalities. I have seen clients that had one personality that was completely dedicated to serving Satan and the coven they were in, while at the same time, having an alternate personality that was entirely devoted to the Lord Jesus Christ and his church. It may sound confusing but it is actually very simple when you understand the mechanics of the mind.[297] The Christian personality will come to you with spiritual problems that they cannot break free from. The problem is not with them but lies in them having another personality that is involved in the worship of devils. In these

---

[297] For a better understanding on the subject I have written the book, "The Big Book on Dissociate Identity Disorder."

cases you will need to rely on the wisdom and leading of the Lord God. Ask God to lead you in how to deal with the person. To be quite honest if you do have a client with DID, I recommend that you bring in a person that has experience in successfully working with dissociates and let them work on the client. Often they will let you sit in on the sessions and will train you at the same time. Once again if you are unfamiliar with working with those with DID, I would strongly recommend studying under someone who has successfully worked with DID. I have written a book on the subject called, "The Big Book on Dissociate Identity Disorder." It is an exhaustive work that covers everything from how the mind works and dissociative states happen to how to help the client come to healing. May the Lord richly bless you in all your endeavors to serve Him.

    In Christ's love: Pastor Tom Knotts, Jr.